"*From Under the Russian Snow* reflects in its title a symbol of the awakening of Russia, the time of hope, expectation and enthusiasm of the people who had never experienced freedom. Michelle Carter came to Russia at this turbulent and exciting period and generously shared with us her knowledge of how to shed the mental fetters of the past. Michelle was not an outsider or just a visitor; she was one of us. She is a talented educator, sensitive and understanding woman and a keen observer. The book she has written depicts with love and sympathy the attempts to build a new Russia. It's about love, life and tragedy—hers and ours."

— Anna Sharogradskaya, Director, Regional
Press Institute, St. Petersburg, Russia

"Michelle Carter's writing is always crisp and evocative, and her work with the children of Chernobyl was nothing less than heroic."

— Congresswoman Jackie Speier (CA-14)

"I know that you have come to the close of your time as professional-in-residence at the Russian-American Press and Information Center and will shortly return to the United States. I would like to take this opportunity to thank you for the many contributions you have made during your tenure at RAPIC toward bettering Russian journalists' understanding of how a free press works in a democratic society. The book you just published on newspaper design and layout is an impressive result of your time in Russia.

"I would also like to thank you for your dedication to your position, despite the enormous loss you suffered this summer. During a time of personal tragedy, you remained committed to your work here. That is both remarkable and truly commendable . . ."

— Thomas R. Pickering, Ambassador to
Russia, Embassy of the United States,
Moscow, Russia, November 14, 1995

Other books by Michelle A. Carter

Children of Chernobyl : Raising Hope from the Ashes

From Under
the Russian Snow

From Under the Russian Snow

by Michelle A. Carter

BInk *Bink Books*
Bedazzled Ink Publishing Company • Fairfield, California

978-1-945805-44-8 paperback
978-1-945805-45-5 epub
978-1-945805-46-2 mobi

Map
by
Ezra Lux

Cover Design
by
Michelle Carter
&

The flower on the cover is the podsnezhnik, the first flower to
appear in the spring in Russia. A symbol of hope and renewal, it
translates to "under the snow."

Bink Books
a division of
Bedazzled Ink Publishing Company
Fairfield, California
http://www.bedazzledink.com

For Laurie

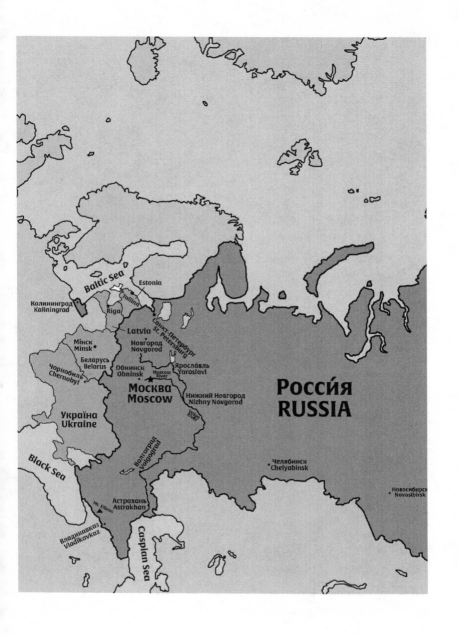

Магадан
Magadan

Россия
RUSSIA

Хабаровск
Khabarovsk

Томск
Tomsk

Lake
Baikal

Владивосток
Vladivostok

The cities Michelle visited during her Great Adventure in Russia.

Acknowledgements

This book was nearly stillborn so many times over the past twenty years as I struggled to find my voice. It would have remained lifeless this time if not for the resuscitations of so many who were ready to lend their skills to the effort.

Because this is a true story populated by generous people who opened their lives to me, I must begin by thanking them for their warm embraces for this aging *Amerikanka* who stumbled about on their turf. Without Anna Sharogradskaya, Oleg and Elena Tumin, Imbi Reet Kaasik and Tanya Patina, I would have had no story to tell. Tanya, in particular, vetted every word of this manuscript to make sure that all my Russian references and my transliterated spellings from the Cyrillic were accurate and consistent.

The best editor any memoirist could have was my daughter Robyn, a published short story writer, who read this book chapter-by-chapter, returning each one with detailed notations to give literary form to my story. My son David pushed me (kicking and screaming) into an honest look at the relationships that shaped this book, and Laurie, of course, gave me the greatest gift of all—his blessing for this Great Adventure.

I've saved a long and loving embrace for my husband, Mike Venturino, who molded the wreckage after Laurie's death into a vibrant second life that includes our grandson Ezra Lux, a third-generation writer and the designer of the map of Russia in this book!

Former *San Mateo Times* colleagues Ro Logrippo and Mike Spinelli shared their unique gifts as well. Ro is a marketing guru without peer, and photographer Mike took the glam photo of me used in all our promotion materials.

I would have had a lovely tale to tell—and nothing more—without C.A. Casey and Claudia Wilde of Bedazzled Ink Publishers, who found, in this story, a book worthy of print. Their confidence in women authors in general, and this one in particular, is no small blessing.

And, of course, an enormous thank you to the cadre of friends across the planet, who are helping to spread the word.

Spasibo za pomosht!

Introduction

My life has unfolded like an M.C. Escher graphic of doors, doors that open into other doors. Each door presents a choice: Open it and walk through, open it and peek inside, or just walk on by. Mostly I walk through them, often with more gusto than grace.

I'm basically nosy, a trait I'm convinced made me a good reporter. I want to know what's next, what's just beyond, what questions need asking. The first in the series of doors that led to my Great Adventure in Russia in 1995 opened into Mr. Tucker's first-year Russian class that I took on a dare as a junior at Proviso East High School in suburban Chicago. I'd had two years of Latin (enough, surely), and the Soviet launch of Sputnik had just stunned the world. So why not Russian?

That class (and five more years of study in high school and college) morphed me into a Russophile of the first order—who did nothing significant with it for nearly thirty years.

Then, at age forty-four, I was invited to participate in a cultural exchange with the Soviet Peace Committee. After a lifetime immersion in Russian history and literature, I got the chance to see the country (in all its Cold War finery) first-hand in 1988. I was smitten.

But it wasn't until my second exchange visit in 1990 that the doors in my Russian sequence stood open and beckoning. On that trip we visited a hospital in Minsk in the Soviet republic of Byelorussia, which cared for the Children of Chernobyl, those youngest victims who marched on May Day 1986 under the radioactive fallout of the world's worst technological disaster.

From that experience came my first book, *Children of Chernobyl: Raising Hope From the Ashes* (Augsburg 1993), co-written with Michael Christensen, and the twenty-year Children of Chernobyl Project of Northern California, which provided medicine and supplies for that Byelorussian hospital.

Another door opened when the director of the Russia desk at the United States Information Agency heard about a Russian-speaking newspaper editor who'd written a new book about Chernobyl and thought she might have found her next Professional-in-Residence for the Russian-American Press and Information Center in Moscow. The bounty behind this door would be a harder sell. Would I be willing to leave at home my husband of twenty-seven years, two grown children, and a job I'd walked across hot coals to win to spend a year crisscrossing the eleven time zones of Russia?

I bet a year of my life that I, at age fifty, could have my Great Adventure, midwifing a free press to full flower in an emerging democracy.

But at what cost? I didn't have a clue.

Chapter One

I CLOSED THE door, snapped the deadbolt, and listened to the voices in the hall.

"Michelle, you must close windows when you leave or the wind will blow and the glass will break. And the drapes, Michelle. Close them to block the sun."

Beyond the door, my landlady and her son were still chattering, in Russian, still reminding me to turn off the gas and set the safety lock when I left the building, still worrying about turning over their apartment to this American woman who had come to Moscow alone, without her family. I was only getting every third word or so, but they had repeated themselves often enough, complete with demonstrations, that I knew what they were saying.

Still, I loved to hear them say my name. Russians pronounced "Michelle" with a soft, rolling "l" at the end, and it sounded much more elegant in Russian than it did in English. And as often as my landlady repeated it, she must have liked to say it, too.

I shouted after them, "I will, I will,"—just about the limit of my Russian after more than twenty-four hours of travel.

Then the doors to the lift clanked shut, the voices ceased, and I really was alone. I turned around slowly. There, leaning against the cushioned Naugahyde of the door of my flat, I could see into all three rooms of the apartment.

I could see past the toilet (in a separate European-style "water closet") and bathroom, through the cozy kitchen and out the tall double casement windows into the inky night. The kitchen, with its tiny table in the corner and Harvest Gold German refrigerator/freezer, looked cozy rather than cramped.

I could see the "western" double bed that all but filled the bedroom. With the addition of the free-standing wardrobe and a low cupboard that would serve as a dresser, moving-around space was limited. But again, those lovely windows would bring the outside into the room.

I could see to the left into the largest room where an exquisite Persian carpet in vibrant reds and blues lay over polished wood parquet (and smell the faint residue of a new coat of floor wax). Beyond that, the stacks of packing boxes that had arrived with me filled every bit of free space.

So this would be the setting for my Great Adventure.

I had imagined this flat every night for the past two months, but this modest two-room apartment was far better than I had allowed myself to hope for. I walked into the living room and sat on one of the boxes.

High, ten-foot ceilings and the windows created a feeling of spaciousness, and double (inside and outside) doors led to a small balcony although now both doors were taped shut against the shrill winds that whipped off the Moscow River. I could tolerate the wallpaper; it was far too "prettified" for my taste with its rows of nosegays marching from floor to ceiling, but I had seen much worse.

The orange sateen drapes were an assault to the senses, but they were standard decorator items in every Russian apartment I'd been in. Muscovites bought them by the yard from state shops and the only variation in the cheap, synthetic fabric was in the color. The shiny gray ones in the bedroom were about as subdued as you could get. Perhaps I could take them down without upsetting the landlady.

However, even the drapes seemed trivial when I considered the one genuine treasure in the flat—a piano with "K. Oppenheimer, Petrograd" lettered in gold over the yellowing keyboard. The label served as a date stamp of sorts for the piano, an ebony upright, since St. Petersburg was called Petrograd only from 1914 (when "Petersburg" sounded too German for World War I sentiments) until the mid-twenties when Leningrad took its place. An old-fashioned piano stool that twisted to the right height completed the ensemble.

There had been a piano in every place Laurie and I had lived after we moved out of the ant-ridden apartment in San Francisco near Golden Gate Park where we "camped" for the first three months of our married life. (From the bay window, we could eavesdrop on the passing crowds of flower children on the street below us who would create the Summer of Love in just a few months.)

For the first few years the pianos were rented, but no matter. Laurie needed the outlet that music provided. He'd come from a musical family (his mother was an accomplished pianist and organist), and he had taken piano lessons on and off for most of his school years. After we were married, the piano provided the transition he seemed to need between work and family life. While I would make dinner, he would play—mostly popular or light classical pieces like Gershwin's *Rhapsody in Blue* or *Lara's Theme* from *Dr. Zhivago*. Listening to him play while I put dinner on the table was as stress-releasing for me as it seemed to be for him.

In fact, the piano played a role in bringing us together as seniors at the University of Missouri in Columbia. Laurie lived in the Sigma Chi house on campus, a big red-brick, white-columned fraternity house and, after three years in residence halls, I had just moved into a little white stucco off-campus house on a lot that abutted the Sigma Chi parking lot. One hot, late summer day before classes started, Laurie knocked on the door of my house while my roommates and I were moving in.

"You wouldn't have an extra throw rug you don't need, would you? I'm living in the basement of the Sigma Chi house next door. It's pretty damp, and I could really use a rug."

I didn't have one, but I thought that was a pretty original "opener" and accepted his invitation to a mixer at the house a few days later.

This tall, rumpled guy with bent glasses had gone to grade school and high school in Kansas City with another Missouri class-mate of mine who had endless stories about Laurie's goofiness and wacky charm, about how he'd once pulled the bathroom sink out of the wall at her house by sitting on it and how he kept getting his glasses knocked off when he played varsity basketball so the coach choreographed specific plays so Laurie really would know where the ball was without having to "see" much.

I didn't expect anything more from the evening than a chance to peek inside this antebellum mansion across the parking lot from my new home. But as I wandered around the house, Laurie lumbered over to the grand piano in the living room, spun down the piano stool to accommodate his long body, and began playing Beatles songs.

The party moved to the piano and, when I joined the crowd singing along, Laurie segued into "Michelle." I wasn't sure he even knew I was a "Michelle" since I'd been introduced as "Micki." (Of course, he later swore he did.) But I went home more than a little interested in this tall, slightly geeky piano guy from Kansas City who seemed to be a most unlikely Sigma Chi—so unlikely in fact that, when we got pinned on my birthday in December, he had to borrow a fraternity pin. He'd never bothered to buy one.

But we always had a piano.

I ran my fingers over the oiled surface of the piano and thought, yes, it will do just fine. Here I would make my home for most of the next year, 10,000 miles away from my family, my friends, from the newspaper where I had made my career for the past twenty-seven years.

The agony of making the decision to come here was well behind me then. This was the first week in January; my husband and I had spent most of the previous fall talking over all the dimensions, all the implications, of such a watershed change in our lives.

"This won't be like other trips when I was part of a big, noisy group. I'll be alone for most of each day," I said.

"I'll be in Stockton working on the warehouse project so you'd be alone here too," he said. "And we've got Oleg and Tanya in Moscow. You'll be able to connect with them whenever you want."

"What if my Russian isn't good enough?"

"Think how good it will be when you get home."

"What if you need me?"

"We always need each other, but I'm a big boy. I may even learn to cook!"

As I replayed some of those discussions still one more time, I walked into the kitchen, leaned against the wide windowsill, and stared out into the night. The glowing street lights reflected on the ice of the river below me. My breath fogged up the window pane but it didn't matter. I wasn't looking in front of me; I was looking back.

THE INVITATION CAME out of the blue. The phone message from Sandra Murphy was among a stack of "While you were out" slips in my in-box when I returned to my office at *The San Mateo Times* after my August vacation. I had led a group to the Chernobyl region of Belarus, the former Soviet republic most seriously damaged by the 1986 nuclear explosion at Chernobyl in the neighboring republic of Ukraine. I'd been doing this once or twice a year since founding the Children of Chernobyl Project of Northern California after my 1990 visit to the Soviet republic of Byelorussia where I'd had one of those life-altering experiences that seemed to be almost routine for me lately.

I had never heard of Sandra Murphy, and the message didn't offer a hint of who she was or what she wanted. The number was long-distance, and I thought I recognized the area code as Washington, D.C. The note settled at the bottom of the pile.

It was a couple of days later when she called again and identified herself as manager of the Russia desk of the United States Information Agency. It took her awhile to get to the point, but she caught my interest when she mentioned my Chernobyl book. (Funny how that works!).

She'd been at a cocktail party and, amid the usual party patter, she had mentioned that she was looking for a newspaper editor with experience in Russia. A woman in the group happened to have been a San Francisco Bay Area television personality who had interviewed me when *Children of Chernobyl* had been published the year before. She told Sandra I sounded like the person she wanted.

Wanted for what?

"I'm looking for someone to spend ten months in Russia as the USIA Journalist-in-Residence at the Russian-American Press and Information Center in Moscow," she said. "Someone who would work with newspaper editors across Russia to ease their rough transition from a controlled media to a free and independent press."

I remember gripping the receiver. Here was an opportunity to combine two of the passions of my life—journalism and Russia, a place that had occupied a corner of my being since I was a high school student studying Russian on a lark.

Was I interested?

Of course, I told her. But it just isn't anything I could even consider. I've worked all my life to get where I am today, the managing editor of a daily newspaper. And I love it! Surely it doesn't come any better than getting up every morning and making a newspaper!

I was a woman succeeding in a world dominated by men, and I loved community newspapering. I felt I was making a difference on the San Francisco Peninsula.

Besides, I was very comfortable in my personal life. My marriage of twenty-seven years was a strong one. My children, in their early twenties, were just beginning their separate lives. They might not have needed me very much, but I surely needed them. And, as a woman of a certain age (soon to be fifty!), I should have been weighing the pros and cons of hormone therapy rather than launching a Great Adventure.

Despite my protests, I suspect Sandra knew she had me from that first phone conversation, but she graciously accepted my refusals.

"I understand, but I wish you'd think it over. Talk to your husband. Perhaps he could even go with you. Could I call you again in a few days?"

She could.

That night, and for many nights after, Laurie and I talked—over dinner, sitting up against pillows in bed, and then in whispers as we cuddled together under the covers when I savored the comfort of his size and gentleness. Laurie was the most supportive husband a strong-willed woman like me could hope for. I'm sure he would have said he would be there for me even if I had told him I wanted to spend ten months in outer space. He was the perfect husband for a woman who tended to be single-minded and headstrong; he was loving, non-judgmental, non-competitive.

One of my favorite stories focused on the time he accompanied me to the American Society of Newspaper Editors conference in Washington, D.C., the previous April. Whenever we would join a social group at a reception or a meal, the editors (almost always men) would start talking newspapers to Laurie, assuming he was the editor of the pair. So he took his nametag out of its plastic slip and wrote, "She's the one!" under his name.

He was the least demanding person I've ever met, and we'd learned early in our marriage not to keep score.

When we'd moved to the San Francisco Peninsula a few months after our January 1967 wedding, we'd agreed that we would both make our careers there. We loved the Bay Area and the nearby Sierra

Nevada Mountains. He had spent his entire youth in Kansas City; I had moved around a lot as a child and both of us wanted stability of place for our children. So we made a pact—neither of us would accept job changes or promotions that would take us away. And we didn't. We stayed, raising our children and settling in. We were nesters, and nesters didn't do the kind of thing that Sandra Murphy was asking.

But I suspect Laurie sensed a restlessness in me that I hadn't yet acknowledged myself. One day he came home with a bouquet of flowers that he had bought at the train station on the way home—something he did from time to time—and handed them to me as he bent to kiss me.

"I think you should do it," he whispered as we hugged. "This is an opportunity that may never come again, a door that may never be open again, and it was made for you. This is the direction your life has been moving for several years now; it's the logical next step.

"Ten months is a long time, but you'll get to come home and I'll go to Moscow—maybe even a couple of times. It'll be over before we know it, and I'll be here when you get back."

That last phrase has echoed in my mind, bounced off the walls of my skull, thousands of times since he said it. That first night in Moscow I was hanging on that promise.

ALTHOUGH I WAS exhausted (it was nearly thirty hours since I'd left home in San Mateo), I was sure it would be hours before I could sleep. I hung up my new navy blue winter coat with the double rows of brass buttons in the hall closet, picked off a few white blonde hairs from the collar, and set my soggy California boots near the radiator under the window in the kitchen.

I glanced at my watch—which I'd reset to Moscow time at the airport—and calculated the correct time in San Mateo. At home, it was eleven hours earlier and I hadn't yet learned the quick computation formula I would use ever after: Back up twelve hours (7 p.m. to 7 a.m.) and add one hour (to arrive at 8 a.m. at home). Nonetheless I determined that Laurie would be up and about to leave for work so I'd better hurry to place my first call home.

The phone in the flat was working. The landlady had told me to dial "eight" for an international line, wait for the tone, and "ten" for the U.S. and then my number, but I was skeptical. I'd never had much faith in Russian telephones, and up until the past year or two, all overseas calls from Russia had to be placed at the local post office.

"Not a problem, not a problem," she had said as she ran her finger around the rotary on the red plastic phone that scooted across the table with each turn of the dial. "It works very well."

Well, now I would really find out. I anchored the phone between my knees and dialed the "eight" and waited until I got a new and different tone. Then the "ten," the San Francisco area code and the number which had been ours for twenty-five years.

Laurie answered on the first ring and his voice came across clearly.

"Hi, honey, I'm here in my own flat and everything's fine," I replied, struggling to eliminate the quavering in my voice. No need, however; he could barely hear me through an annoying echo, and I had to repeat the same sentence three times before he could understand. I wanted to be reassuring and confident, but the entire conversation was reduced to shouted phrases: "Couldn't sleep . . . snowing . . . nice apartment . . . very safe."

Finally, I gave up. "I love you . . . very much. . . Miss you . . . Tell the kids . . . I'll send an e-mail . . . Remember, I love you . . . Bye."

It wasn't the conversation I'd been longing for. My hands were shaking as I put down the phone, which reminded me of a child's toy since it had none of the heft and authority of western telephones. It also wasn't going to provide an acceptable substitute for human contact when I would need it in the coming months. Somehow I'd been counting on the telephone if things got too shaky, but if this first experience was the norm, that was one support system I couldn't depend on.

My feelings were an unsettled mix of fear, exhilaration, and loneliness, and I was verging on nausea as I unpiled the boxes in the living room. I was looking for the one with the notation: "Open first."

As I slit the taped edges with the only dinner knife in the kitchen, I laughed out loud, remembering how afraid I'd been that some Customs official would want me to open the boxes at Sheremyetevo

Airport in Moscow. But, as it turned out, I had more things to worry about then than an arrogant Russian bureaucrat.

SANDRA MURPHY HAD promised me a VIP greeting. "You won't have to lift a single box. They will meet you as soon as you come through Passport Control and then they'll escort you through Customs and into the van. Stop worrying about those boxes."

But I didn't believe her. I had arrived at Sheremyetevo a dozen times before and no one had ever provided a VIP greeting. I'd always had to schlep my own bags before. I also practiced my own preaching—never "*expect*" anything in Russia except the unexpected. So I had packed the boxes to be light enough for me to lift without straining my sometimes cranky back. That's why it took so many. There were fifteen boxes and bags, but not one weighed more than forty pounds.

I knew the ex-pat American kids who worked at the RAPIC office would be rolling on the floor at the idea of my hauling fifteen pieces to Russia, but I needed to surround myself with everything necessary to make a home here. I planned to cook and bake and entertain, to nest, to put down some roots here.

And they were fifteen not-so-big, relatively light boxes, after all.

As I stood in line in the dim forty-watt light of Passport Control, I stretched to my full five-feet-eight inches in search of someone holding a sign with my name on it. No one waiting; no signs. How about someone resembling a porter? Not likely.

The baggage carousel was already wheezing and chugging when I emerged, and by then I knew I had been wise to pack lightly. I dug into my purse for my ruble stash which I'd secreted away last August and put down sixteen hundred rubles for four rickety, highly unstable baggage carts. I shepherded all four to the baggage carousel, slung my purse across my body and went to work like a longshoreman.

I'd plastered each bag and box with numbered labels so I was ready to wrestle each one off the conveyor belt and onto one of the carts. Within thirty minutes, I had all four carts piled high, and I surveyed the Customs lines. I opted for the nearest line with one very tired looking inspector.

One after another, I lined up my four teetering carts of five medium-sized boxes, three suitcases, six small boxes, and a portable computer and pushed them toward him one at a time. Each time the line inched forward, I moved up each of my four carts, one at a time. Finally, it was my turn. I pushed the first cart to the counter, plopped down my passport and Customs declaration and started to bring up the next cart.

He pushed the documents back at me and laughed. "You've been working hard. You deserve a rest."

Then he shoved open the gate and motioned me through with a grand and mocking bow. Not even a notoriously suspicious Russian Customs inspector would step in front of this woman on a mission and her four carts of luggage.

My VIP greeting did await me—in the public reception area—in the form of twenty-five-year-old Renny Hart from the Press Center and a strong-backed young driver. We pushed the carts to the waiting van (only two trips this time!), and I crawled in and collapsed in the back seat for the long ride into the center of the city.

But the boxes had made it to their destination, and my back was no worse for wear.

CAREFULLY, I REMOVED the sheets that I'd used to protect the framed photos I knew I would want as soon as I was alone in my flat. I took out one of Laurie and me at Point Lobos on the Monterey Peninsula, one of my son David playing guitar with an orange and white tabby cat on his lap, one of my daughter Robyn looking pensive and uncharacteristically fragile in the kitchen of our San Mateo home. The last image was one of my goddaughter Amy hugging her dad, Paul.

Amy's photo had been wrapped in an exquisite brown and gold silk shawl with deep fringe. It had belonged to my dearest friend Bette, Amy's mom, who had died of breast cancer the previous August. I wrapped the shawl around me and twisted my fingers in the fringe. Bette's death had been wrenching—and beautiful. She had known since May that her cancer had returned and invaded her spine despite her mastectomy three years earlier, and she had decided that her remaining time would not be marginalized by desperation chemotherapy. She had planned her death in a way that she had not been able to do with her life. While she was still strong and looking great, she arranged for hospice workers to come to her house and explain what lay ahead for her. She would stay at home and die at home.

In late July she summoned her sisters to come to California and spend a week in Carmel with her. She shopped for a swimsuit that would disguise her bloated stomach and huge sunglasses to hide the circles under her eyes for that last reunion, and they were all laughing together at the rented beach house when she started having trouble breathing. The E.R. doctor said it was time so her sisters brought her home where she died five days later surrounded by her husband, children, parents, brother, and sisters.

During those five days, I had had the chance to say my goodbyes. Mostly I just sat and held her hand while she drifted in and out of consciousness and thought about the injustice of a young life cut short. There really were no guarantees in life. None at all.

Perhaps I was more ready to get Sandra Murphy's call than I ever realized. No one knew what lay in store for me or any of us. Why not a Great Adventure for me?

A door slamming in the next flat jolted me awake. I had fallen asleep wrapped in Bette's shawl, sitting on one box and leaning against another. I carried the sheets into the bedroom, undressed, and fell instantly asleep on the bare mattress, burrowed under a down comforter and two of those huge, square European pillows.

An unfamiliar flat, white light filled the room when I awoke. It wasn't like sunshine, more like a huge fluorescent lamp burning outside the window. The quality of the light deepened the intensity of that "Where am I?" sensation that floods over you when you wake in a strange place. After several seconds of mental re-orientation, I pulled the comforter around me and pushed back the sateen drapes and sheer curtains at the bedroom window for my first look at all that had been hidden in the darkness the night before.

The curious winter light seemed to be a product of the high, flat overcast that I would come to know well in Russia, along with the fresh snow that covered every surface below me and the slate-colored ice of the Moscow River that dominated the landscape in front of me. That white light would define winter in Moscow for me for months to come, but that first morning, it was discomfiting, so unlike either the morning fog or afternoon sunshine of home, so foreign and far away.

I shouldn't have been shocked to discover that it was ten thirty when I glanced at my watch. I knew that it didn't get light in Moscow in January until nearly ten but I couldn't believe I had slept so long. I was hungry, and all those boxes were waiting. I dug into the "Open First" box and pulled out my well-worn sweats and some socks. Dressed for work, I filled the tea pot with bottled water and set it on the stove. I struck a match to light the burner of the small gas stove. My new life really had begun whether I was ready or not.

I didn't even venture out that first day. I ate some of the food I had brought and spent the entire day unpacking and making a comfortable and homey space out of that two-room flat (Russians don't count kitchens and bathrooms as "rooms"). The framed photos went on the piano, over Bette's fringed shawl, and the teddy bear that had sat on my desk at *The Times* took up a new position on the sofa. I was nesting again, but this time only for myself.

The dark returned by four o'clock but it wasn't until after a dinner of ramen noodles and a breakfast bar that I plugged in my Macintosh PowerBook 140 at the kitchen table and sat down to begin the first of the regular columns, *Letters From Russia*, that I would e-mail back to *The Times*—once I'd figured out how to get online! Thanks to some foresight on Laurie's part, that wasn't as big a deal as I feared. Before we set up an e-mail account for me to use in Russia, we called all the Internet Service Providers until we found one, America Online, which had a local access telephone number and a technical support line in Moscow. Good thing, since the service techs and I got to know each other very well.

We both had set up our first ever personal e-mail accounts with AOL. We had to limit our user name to ten characters so "Micki Carter" became "mickicartr," and I've been explaining that missing "e" ever since.

A year after I returned to California, AOL discontinued its dial-up service in Russia because, they said, Russians were gaining AOL service by fraud; they were typing in sixteen random numbers for credit card accounts until one worked. I was amazed that they had any accounts that weren't fraudulent since Russians had absolutely no access to credit cards, a fact that apparently had escaped the folks in marketing at AOL.

But once I got my modem speaking Russian, we were in business. The clattering of that portable computer keyboard would be a sound forever linked to that apartment by the Moscow River.

The first *Letter From Russia* appeared a week later in *The Times*.

Letters From Russia
Settling in for the year in Moscow

MOSCOW — The sun just broke through the persistent overcast and this dirty, teeming city looks nearly golden.

From my apartment on the Rostov Embankment of the Moscow River, I look across at the massive gingerbread facade of the Kiev railway station. To the right, sitting on one of the many curves of the river, is the Russian White House where the scars of the November 1993 confrontation have been erased and a new golden double-eagle in the tower glistens off the ice.

The apartment, a two-room flat, is very comfortable. With high ceilings and parquet hardwood floors, Oriental carpets and new wallpaper, it's a gem. A polished ebony upright piano with the label "Petrograd"—the revolutionary name of St. Petersburg—dominates the living room and a brand new German refrigerator/freezer shines in the tiny kitchen.

The building itself was constructed in the Fifties when Stalin undertook his redesign of the city which included seven identical "wedding cake" buildings in a variety of sizes that dominate the skyline. Many of those Stalin-era buildings have crumbled into typical examples of Soviet-era ugliness, but this one has had some care.

The lift (elevator) works and a keyless security system has been added at the entry hall, which is pleasant by Russian standards. The door opens onto a private drive in the back and a playground with park benches and a small sledding hill which is full of children despite the zero-degree F weather. A wide, tree-lined parkway stretches between the building and the river, home to the biggest ravens I've ever seen and a clutch of hardy sparrows who rest on my narrow little balcony. I'd feed them, but the door is sealed and taped shut against the winter drafts.

An arching bridge crosses the river carrying traffic to the train station and the boxy and non-descript Slavyanskaya Hotel which has become something of a western enclave in this city with its bank, money exchange and western newspaper stand—a pricey hotel with very pricey toys—but a place where homesick Americans can be sure to hear English spoken with softened American edges. The bridge itself, however, is to be avoided by non-Muscovites at all costs, so I'm told. Hordes of Gypsy children frequent the steps from time to time and set upon the unsuspecting, lifting wallets, passports, and jewelry in an instant. The warnings no doubt are sincere, but I can see the entire bridge and steps from my flat, and I haven't seen a horde of any sort, children or adults. Maybe it's not the season for tourists or Gypsy children.

Two of those multi-layered "wedding cakes" define my neighborhood. At night, the illuminated and crenellated tower of the Ukraina Hotel dominates the skyline from my kitchen window. After an earlier trip to the former Soviet Union, I considered writing the thinnest book ever—a volume on all the clean public restrooms in the USSR—and the Ukraina could claim the only one I'd ever found. Now, thanks to McDonalds and Pizza Hut, they are proliferating all over Moscow like German appliances and neon signs. And clean restrooms represent a heritage far more durable than Big Macs and French fries.

The other "wedding cake" nearby is the Ministry of Foreign Affairs where pimply-faced seventeen-year-olds rest Kalashnikov rifles on their arms as they lean against the doorways in the central courtyard. I'll probably begin to recognize their faces soon. That courtyard is the first thing I see as I emerge from the pedestrian undercrossing at my Metro station—and I've already begun to think of it as mine, along with my embankment, my sparrows, and my market.

For an ex-patriate (sounds rather romantic, doesn't it?) and a Californian at that, I'm settling into Moscow's winter routine rather well. I haven't yet adjusted to the sun coming up at 10 and setting at 4 or sidewalks with six inches of ice, but I'm learning to take those short sliding steps that Russians use to get around.

Today the sun shone brightly; as long as that happens once every ten days or so, I'll be fine.

Chapter Two

HUGE BANNERS SALUTING the New Year (*Noviy God*) still hung from the buildings near my flat on Orthodox Christmas, three days after I arrived, and I was reminded that New Year's was still the most significant—and commercial—of the holidays in Russia.

In the Soviet Union, which was officially atheistic, all the symbols of Western Christmas had been co-opted for New Year's. Two- and three-foot evergreen trees (usually artificial) were decorated and hung with tinsel in nearly every flat. Gifts were exchanged at midnight on New Year's Eve when the family gathered for a lively, vodka-infused late night meal. Children listened for the jingling bells that would signal the arrival of Grandfather Frost and the Snow Maiden— whose main role, it seemed, was to help an unsteady Grandfather Frost along after he'd been toasted at every home they visited.

Christmas is observed on January 7, according to the old Julian calendar the Russian Orthodox Church still operates by, as a singularly religious event, with all-night communion and candlelight services at Orthodox cathedrals all over Russia. Even though the Soviets sucked all the political power out of the church, shuttered many of the cathedrals, and persecuted the clergy, Orthodoxy managed to eke out an existence. But in the last few years of Soviet power, a resurgent church had been gaining strength and position; it was perfectly poised to reassume its authority as the official church of Russia when the USSR collapsed.

That focus on New Year's as a purely secular holiday wasn't a bad idea, I remember thinking. Why not pack all the commercialism of gift-buying and gift-giving into a state holiday and save Christmas for the religious event that it is. That's one Soviet notion that would have a lot of takers in the U.S.

On the chance that I might never have another opportunity for two Christmases in one year, I decided to go to an Orthodox service. I skipped Christmas Eve since hours standing on a cold marble floor wasn't particularly appealing, and my personal weather indicator—

the river beneath my window—was frozen solid. But on Christmas morning the sun was shining and some wet spots dotted the surface, so I decided to brave it. I walked through the fresh snow with my face tilted up (to catch every possible ray from the sun) to the small, white stucco church I'd found on a side street not far from my flat.

Even in the brittle cold, the tall, ornate doors stood open because the crowd was spilling out into the courtyard. The monotonal chanting of prayer responses replaced traffic noises as the dominant sound in the neighborhood. I squeezed my way up to the doors and edged into the sanctuary. I staked out a place to stand near a candelabra where the crowd was thinner and stretched to see as much as I could. The only places to sit were the narrow benches along the walls; a sign indicated they were to be reserved for the handicapped and mothers with babies. In fact, no one at all was sitting. Everyone was standing and straining to see the action.

Babushki (grandmothers or elderly women) filled the congregation, but there were plenty of men, children, and young people there as well. A frizzy-bearded priest in gold-embroidered vestments and miter walked the length of the nave swinging an incense censer, part of the "smells and bells" of the Orthodox faith. Wafts of burning cinnamon, anise, and smoking resin from fir trees stung my sinuses and clouded my contacts as the faithful pressed back against the walls to make way.

Just then a bent old crone wrapped in a brown wool scarf reached out and smacked my left arm.

"Be reverent," she hissed at me. "This is the house of God!"

In an effort to make myself small in the crowd, I had stuffed my hands in my coat pockets—a cultural taboo that I should have remembered. This scowling *babushka* would see that I wouldn't forget again.

With my hands folded—reverently—in front of me, I let the sensual elements of the service wash over me. The bell-clear tones of the choir of boy sopranos singing a cappella soared from arched lofts high above, and on either side, of the sanctuary. Confessors kissed the golden Bible cover as they mumbled their sins, and the priests scooped sacramental wine and floating bits of bread into the mouths of squalling babies with an ornate silver spoon.

A young couple moved to the left side of the sanctuary in front of the gate that defined the holy space (where only the clergy could go) and held up a baby for baptism. Another much-younger priest emerged from the door in the *iconostasis*, actually a wall of brilliantly illustrated icons, took the infant (rather roughly, I thought), and carried it to a font a few steps away. With a flick of his wrist, he spritzed holy water over the baby's head, murmured something, and handed it back to its parents. The holy sacrament took less than a minute.

Quite suddenly, I realized I was swaying. Still dressed for the frosty morning walk, I was much too warm. My hair was damp under my wool hat, and the stale air, incense, and burning candles left me dizzy and a bit queasy. Despite my overheated body, my feet were numb with cold, and I stumbled on the uneven paving stones in the floor of the church as I tried to move. With one hand on the wall, I pushed through the crowd into the courtyard. I took a deep breath and gasped as the icy air stabbed my lungs.

In my haste, I hadn't backed respectfully out the church door, but this time no *baba* was close enough to slug me for my offense.

BY THE TIME I got home and pulled off my knit hat, I noticed that the tendrils that poked out at my neck and in front of my ears were stiff; they had frozen during the twenty-minute walk home.

"Great!" I said out loud. "I'll probably get pneumonia the first week I'm here."

I dug into the bottom of my wardrobe and pulled out a super-sized jar of chewable vitamin C tablets. I intended to do everything I could to stay well and avoid the need for a doctor in Moscow. I'd brought antibiotics, multiple vitamins, cold medicines, and enough Imodium to start my own *apteka* (pharmacy). My daily health regimen would be strict. I would even floss!

I chewed on the orange-flavored tablets and, once I'd warmed my fingers enough to type, I sat down at my PowerBook and started an e-mail message to Laurie:

Hi, Honey! It's Christmas Day here, and I went to church. It's so cold—minus 10 degrees Celsius—that my hair actually froze. I've heard that the hair in your nose will freeze, too, but I think I was spared that.

However, the apartment is quite comfortable—which is a good thing since I don't have any way to adjust the temperature. The hot water and the radiator are controlled at some bureau in the city—which gives new meaning to central planning, don't you think? But if it gets too warm, the double windows in each room have their own little windows at the top that can be opened. They're called *fortochki*. So, since I like to sleep in a cool room, I just open the *fortochka* before I go to bed, and the down comforter feels wonderful.

Tomorrow is my first day at the office, but there won't be any need to rush in the morning. Regular office hours in Moscow are 10 a.m. to 6 p.m.—probably because so many people have hour-and-a-half to two-hour commutes. And then, of course, it doesn't get light until late. But I'm still waking up at 5 or 6 since my body clock hasn't reset itself yet. I'll be ready for lunch by the time I get to the office!

After tomorrow I'll have a real sense of what the next ten months will be like. Ten months! It sounds like an eternity. I'm sure my homesickness will pass. I keep telling myself it will be like summer camp as a kid. At first you're miserable, but by the time your folks come to get you, you don't want to leave.

I miss you desperately. I've started having those "overachiever" dreams where I know you are in the next room but I can't unlock the door, or I'm trying to call you, but I can't dial the number. In the one last night, I was following you down a long hallway, sort of a tunnel with concrete block walls painted hospital green, and I saw you go into a room and slam the door. I ran to the room and tried to open the door, but it was locked.

I had a bunch of keys on a chain, and I tried one after another, but none of them worked. When someone else came along and opened the door, the room was empty.

Every day I ask myself if I did the right thing by creating this long separation. I hope so, I really hope so. Write soon and tell the kids I'm still waiting for their first e-mails. I live to hear that little chirp, "You've got mail!" when I sign on.

THE INTERNET WAS my lifeline to home, now that I was halfway around the globe, but AOL was a leaky lifeboat at best. I don't know how many times I called that local access number my first few days in Moscow: My Powerbook wouldn't "talk" to AOL, but once I changed my modem settings to "pulse," my Mac and AOL could "shake hands" across cyberspace.

Next, I couldn't stay online long enough to compose anything. Life got a lot less frustrating when I learned about "flash sessions" to download incoming mail and upload mail I'd written offline in, well, a flash!

I was on first-name basis with a tech named Volodya who spoke English about as well as I spoke Russian. He sounded about seventeen, and he was fascinated that I had a Mac. Apple products were pretty scarce in Moscow, so he spent a lot of time e-mailing AOL staff in the U.S. so he could advise me. I suspect my connection problems gave him something quirky to chew on.

Once we had things humming (sort of), AOL announced a major hike in its per-minute rate. The cost of maintaining my lifeline was about to suck up my entire budget. The flash sessions didn't use many minutes but, two or three times a week, the online connection stayed live long after I had quit AOL and gone on to other computer tasks. After two mind-blowing bills from AOL (and some state-side digging by Laurie), I learned that the only way I could actually be sure the modem connection was closed was to shut down my computer after each flash session.

Throughout January and February, every e-mail to Laurie included numbing minutia about expenses all dutifully recorded on Quicken, which we'd loaded onto my laptop. I kept three accounts (dollars, rubles, and credit card charges) and struggled mightily to make them balance—even to the point of listening to the Russian business report on the radio each morning to catch the current ruble-to-dollar exchange rate. I gave that up as soon as I learned that none of the exchanges I used bothered with the "official" rate.

Laurie was meticulous about money. He wasn't cheap, but he didn't like surprises. He kept a loose-leaf binder on his desk in which he added up all our annual expenses (insurance, property taxes, fluctuating utility bills, future purchases like cars and appliances) and then divided them by twelve months. Then, each month, he set aside that amount so that the funds were available when bills came due. We lived off Laurie's salary and, except for the cost of child care, my total salary (which was roughly the same as his) went into savings or investments.

He planned ahead; nothing was an impulse buy. I chafed a bit from time to time, but I wasn't exactly a spendthrift myself. Shortly after he proposed to me (New Year's Day 1966 at the Sugar Bowl in New Orleans when Mizzou beat Florida), he ripped two pieces of paper from a spiral notebook and asked me to write down how much annual income I thought our family would need to live on comfortably. He would do the same, and then we would compare notes. I scribbled ten thousand dollars; so did he. (That's roughly equivalent to forty-nine thousand dollars in 1995, about two-thirds of what we were actually living on.)

While I was still in the hospital after giving birth to Robyn, he bought a twenty-five dollar savings bond and brought it to me. That was the first deposit in her college fund. That grew a thousand-fold before she enrolled at University of California at Santa Cruz and announced to us that she didn't want any of that money. She would pay her own way—and she did, working at the university switchboard and cleaning motel rooms. Something about the acorn not falling far from the oak seems apt here.

Laurie did the same thing three years later when David was born, but David didn't have any ethical issues about accepting the money when he headed for UC Santa Barbara. Same gene set, but very different people.

Laurie's zeal for instilling his organizational and management skills in the kids never diminished. He gave them both checking accounts and plastic file boxes on their twelfth birthdays along with a detailed plan for budgeting. He showed them his loose-leaf binders where he recorded financial transactions and detailed our plans for the future.

The binders were lined up like soldiers at attention on the green metal filing cabinet in our bedroom alongside another labeled (with his Dymo embossed label maker) GOALS. Those goals were specific ("Acquire a vacation place while the kids are young") as well as aspirational ("Learn how to run an effective meeting.") Robyn remembers peeking into that binder from time to time to see if it had been updated. It had been, regularly.

On our fifteenth anniversary, Laurie showed me his latest addition to the GOALS binder: "Take the kids to Europe." We'd have to save up for that one. The kids were sixteen and thirteen before we could set aside three weeks in July for a trip that would begin in Venice and end in London with stops in Rome, Paris, and Zurich. And as you might imagine, our teenagers weren't thrilled with the notion of spending a big chunk of the summer in Europe with their parents. (*National Lampoon's European Vacation* comes to mind.) But Laurie would not be swayed. Even a last minute hiccup—David's all-star baseball team made it to the state finals (to be played while we would all be in Italy)—would not be allowed to disrupt this family trip. I was willing to let David stay with another family and catch a later flight alone, but Laurie was not. We all went—together—and had a wonderful time, dammit!

WHILE I WAS mastering online finance, I picked up another survival skill. One morning I flipped the light switch in the bathroom, and the lights went out—just the overhead lights, not anything plugged into wall outlets (actually floor outlets here). Curious.

I found the fuse box in the hall closet. Two circuits were marked with labels of white tape ("lights" and "outlets"). So I learned that Russian circuitry is built in layers rather than room-by-room as in the U.S. I took out the fuse under "lights" and poked around until I found a cobwebby shoebox of electrical what-not with another fuse that looked something like the one I took out. I unscrewed the one that failed and put the new one in. Nothing. I tapped things and screwed things in and out, absolutely sure I was going to get seriously zapped. Still nothing.

Damn, I would have to call the landlady (who already thought I was a few cards short of a full deck) and slammed the door of the fuse box. The lights flickered. Hmmm. I did it again. Same thing. Now I opened the box just a smidgen to see what was happening when the door slammed. Turns out a little button in the middle of the big, black fuse got pushed in a bit when the door slammed. I pushed the button all the way in and—let there be light! You'd think I'd discovered penicillin, I was so tickled.

I grabbed my journal and recorded exactly what I had done to reset the circuits, tore the page out and tacked it on the wall above the fuse box. The fuses were all loose and crumbling so I would probably need to do this at least once a week.

Even with blown fuses and AOL haggling, I had a lot of empty time on my hands, much more than I could ever remember. To fill the hours, I'd taken to setting specific tasks for myself each day:

- Find a good place to hide cash in the flat. Done! I wrapped the hundred-dollar bills (spotless, without a crease, just as the exchanges here required) in a plastic Ziploc bag, took the ice tray out of the freezer, put the money on the bottom and refilled the tray. So clever of me, but I later learned that western freezers were the first place a self-respecting Moscow burglar looked. Oh, well.
- Figure out how to clean the Oriental carpet in the living room with the stiff broom the landlady left without covering everything else with dust. Easy. I bought a small canister vacuum cleaner (used) at the hardware "corner" of the *rinok* (outdoor market) by the Kiev railroad station and hauled it home in my very cold, very stiff hands with the hose and nozzle dangling over my shoulder and banging my butt with every step.
- Locate a ceiling stud in the foyer and install the smoke-detector Laurie had insisted I pack. Not so easy. I had to drag the tiny kitchen table to a spot just inside the padded Naugahyde door so I had something to stand on. (Those

lovely high ceilings come at a cost.) I tapped the ceiling with
the tack hammer from the toolkit Laurie had assembled and
listened for the solid response of the stud. Crap from the
ceiling kept falling in my eyes (asbestos, no doubt!), but the
crossbeam revealed itself eventually. The screws grabbed
into the wood, and probably the only smoke-detector in
all of Moscow was standing guard.

WHEN I COULDN'T keep busy, I found myself pulled to that
gorgeous piano. I couldn't really play it. A couple months of tortured
accordion lessons when I was six taught me enough to play the right
hand, and I often wished I'd brought a beginner's piano book so I
could have taught myself to play with both hands while I had the time.

But the right hand alone was enough for me to plunk out the
melody from the Caz Chorale sheet music I'd brought along. Caz
Chorale was the folk group at church, led by our friend Mike
Venturino on guitar. We chose mostly Jesuit songs with Woody
Guthrie and Malvina Reynolds thrown in for good measure.

Two weeks before I left for Russia, Caz Chorale (named for our
family camp—Cazadero) gathered at the home of our pastor and his
wife, John and Gretchen Brooke. As a surprise for me, John recorded
our singing and chatter that night, and he handed me the cassette as
we left. That tape would get me through many low moments. I could
sing and play along or just listen. Laurie's voice was distinctive on the
tape. When I needed to hear it, I could.

I have a tin ear, but folk singing isn't too demanding, and I had a
lot of fun with it. Laurie had a clear tenor voice that anchored that
corner of the church choir. He'd been singing in choirs since he was
in kindergarten. I had not—but I thought the church choir was just
the sort of forgiving place where I might learn.

Laurie was not happy. I'd thought he would welcome the chance
for us to do something else together, but he bristled when I told him
I'd talked to the choir director and flat-out refused when I asked for
help. He never explained himself, no matter how much I prodded,
but music had always been something he was good at—and I was
not. As a musician, he had a confidence in himself that he couldn't
muster in other parts of his life so he might have needed this wedge

of separation between us, some place which was his own where he didn't have to deal with me.

Or maybe I just embarrassed him.

I backed off from choir, but not Caz Chorale. Slipping that cassette into my tape recorder and plinking along on the piano when I was on shaky ground lifted me up when nothing else could.

I STILL HAD a weekend to kill, so why not try a solo adventure? I'd take the Metro across town to Izmailovo, the outdoor market where you could buy honest-to-goodness Uzbek carpets or knock-off KGB flasks and everything in between. Outdoor, you say, in January? Well, yes, that was part of the charm. I looked like the Michelin man, layered for warmth, as I headed for Smolenskaya station to present my just-purchased monthly Metro pass and start my journey out to the northeast corner of the city. I was far too hot on the ride, but barely warm enough for wandering the stalls under that wispy pink winter sky.

A girl about seven, in fingerless mitts and so bundled that only her dark empty eyes and thick lashes were showing, drew her bow across untuned strings on her violin, busking just outside the gate, while her mother hovered nearby. I had seen her there every time I'd come, but this time she earned the fistful of rubles I tossed in her violin case for showing enough grit to be there at all.

The *shashlik* vendors were grilling skewers of lamb off to one side, and the enticing charred meat smells had already drawn crowds of shoppers who hunched over tables, made from up-ended cable spools, with their backs to the wind. My stomach was making noisy demands, but I'd wait to treat myself on the way out. I'd tucked a Tupperware box in my "perhaps" bag with the *shashliki* in mind.

The zero-degree weather hadn't made much of a dent in the horde of Saturday shoppers who were, by and large, locals pushing past the Yeltsin and Gorbachev *matryoshki* dolls in search of water filters and second-hand power tools. Over the years, I'd collected all the enameled pins and malachite bracelets that I would ever need, but I still had a soft spot in my heart for the beautiful lacquered *papier-mâché* boxes with the fairy tale figures painted on top. I'd learned how to tell the real ones from the rip-offs (look for brush strokes instead of decals), and I picked through several displays until I found a keeper (red lacquer with the Firebird on the lid) that would rest on Bette's scarf on the piano for the rest of my stay.

I intended to use it as a jewelry box for the gold-and-red enameled pin in the shape of a rosebud that Laurie had given me as a graduation present the year before we were married. However, I almost never took it off. I'm wearing it in nearly all the snapshots I have from my year in Russia.

Heading back to the gate at Izmailova, I lost my way in all the winding alleys and stumbled upon the booth of a young woman who painted gorgeous pastel eggs with the delicate faces of Russian peasant girls. They were lovely and not too expensive (about ten dollars each). I flashed on a Christmas tree decorated with these and chose three to nestle in my bag with the red lacquer Firebird box.

I window-shopped among the rug merchants, brushing off their make-an-offers with my just-lookings and eavesdropping on the price wrangling of other shoppers. An intricately patterned rug from one of the 'Stans (former Soviet republics of Uzbekistan, Kyrgyzstan, Kazakhstan, Turkmenistan, Tajikistan) with a bit of a musky scent (camel?) and big enough for my San Mateo dining room, I over-heard, could be had for about a hundred dollars.

Ah, all those boxes I hauled off the carousel at the airport would not go home half-empty after all!

Letters From Russia
Learning to walk all over again

MOSCOW — Getting around in Russia takes skills I didn't know I had and others I'm sure I'll never learn.

For my entire adult life, ice has been nothing more than something to avoid on the ski slopes by lingering longer over morning coffee in the lodge. Now it's my daily adversary.

As soon as I push back the covers in the morning, I go to the window to check the density of the ice on the river just across the embankment: No ice—only one layer under my coat; ice floes—two layers and socks inside the leather boots; a solid sheet—pile on everything I own and get out the bulky snow boots.

But the ice on the sidewalks is not so easy to define—or even find. A fresh snowfall or even temperature above freezing doesn't diminish the treachery of the ice; all it does is hide it under a dirty crush or a glaze of water and give you false confidence.

Actually the new snow isn't so bad. The word for beginners around here is "head for the white." Unsullied snow provides the best footing and, if you can find a patch, that's your safest footfall. But that inch or two of standing water, when the temperature climbs above freezing, can be a killer.

First you have to understand that few sidewalks in this city ever get shoveled. A good friend of mine who has lived here for years and speaks fluent Russian noted that he didn't know the Russian word for "shovel." It's a relatively new phenomenon even to find snow shovels in the stores. But thanks to the new western shops opening on the boulevards, shoveling the sidewalk in front of your business is gaining converts. If you can stay on the broad shopping streets, you can pick your way across the unshoveled patches to get to the long stretches of good footing.

But on the side streets, all bets are off. Shoveling (or sweeping the snow with a twig broom) is the responsibility of the individual building custodians. Despite orders from the ever-ambitious mayor of

Moscow, those who actually wield the shovels or brooms do much as they please. The front stoop of my building is usually free of snow, but the sidewalk looms icy and treacherous at the foot of it.

Even if all custodians and businesses were diligent at clearing the sidewalks, some quirks of construction around here are out to defeat the best efforts. For starters, the downspouts come down the sides of buildings and, instead of running under the sidewalk and pouring water into the street, they dump water out onto the sidewalk at the base of the building. So, with the constant melting and freezing, small mounds of ice form at the bottom of the downspouts that can be removed only with back-busting chipping. And when those mounds are wet, look out!

Such an ice mound was my undoing last week. The sun had shone most of the day, and I could feel its warmth on my back as I walked to a meeting in a building a few blocks away. But on my way back, the sun had set, and everything that had melted under the daytime's sunny gaze was quickly freezing over.

The dark, of course, adds still another dimension to the threat. I didn't see the ice mound, and down I went. I must admit it was a fairly graceful baseball slide, and I managed to land with some dignity—and no damage, thanks to the usual layers of clothing. I found a foothold and got to my feet without so much as a glance to my fellow walkers who had noted the spot and were giving it wide berth.

Once I was safely home, I found myself wishing for colder weather so, at least, I wouldn't have the water glaze to deal with. However, the irony of my wishing for a freeze (when I spend my entire existence bundled up) didn't escape me. I had a good laugh as I pulled off my boots.

Now I know what people here mean when they say, "Don't waste your wishes on March." March, so I'm told, is an entire month of muddy, freeze/melt misery. Oh well, at least the days will be longer.

So I walk with my eyes on the path in front of me, measuring the possible depth of the muddy puddles, with quick glances at the traffic approaching from all sides. Pedestrians are not a protected species in Moscow; they're fair game—especially when the walkers take to the streets to avoid the icy sidewalks. I could pass my own daughter on the street and not even notice because walking takes all my concentration. That may explain why westerners always note that Russians never smile on the streets. It has nothing to do with friendliness; they're just concentrating on walking.

Most of the time I feel I should have a big blue "L" (for "learner") on my back the way the cars of student drivers are marked in some parts of the country. I'm definitely a "learner walker" on the streets of Moscow.

My California boots aren't much help either. The sand and salt that's thrown on the ice does precious little for the footing, but it eats leather alive. In my first care package from home, I asked for shoe polish and waterproof spray. Now my daily ritual includes wiping my boots clean and putting them near the radiator so they will dry completely overnight. Then on weekends, they get polished and waterproofed—out of the probably vain hope that they will survive through the rest of the winter.

And how long's that? A Russian will tell you that this country has only two seasons—two months of summer and ten months of waiting for summer. I guess I'll be waiting for a good while yet.

Chapter Three

THE SURFACE OF the ice on the river showed significant cracks Monday morning when I made my way to my first day of work along the icy sidewalks of the Garden Ring, the broad, traffic-glutted boulevard (where lanes are just a suggestion!) that circles Moscow's city center. The warm spell made navigating the streets even more treacherous since a film of water could hide some nasty—and super slippery—ice underneath.

But at least I wouldn't get lost. The day before, hand-drawn map in hand, I'd scouted the best route from my flat to the two-story yellow building in the neighborhood of once-posh nineteenth century homes near Stariy Arbat (Old Arbat) Street. That cobblestoned street, open only to pedestrians now, is lined with lovely old pastel-colored mansions that once housed artists, writers, and musicians. Both Alexander Pushkin and Leo Tolstoy had owned grand houses here. Now the majority of the buildings were in varying stages of renovation—in fact, most of Moscow is under *remont*—to shake off seventy years of Soviet neglect and make room for all the restaurants and shops that have turned the street into a major tourist draw.

The building that housed the Russian-American Press and Information Center (RAPIC) sits on Khlebniy Pereulok, one of the maze of narrow side streets that yield sightseeing gems for the visitors who venture off the main thoroughfares. In these two- and three-story mansions with carriage entrances, bowed front windows and wrought-iron balconies, the noble families that served the tsars made their homes. The streets are even named to indicate the type of service provided. "*Khlebniy*" was home to the bread-makers; the next street over was the province of those who washed and ironed the table linens.

RAPIC occupied the smaller of two matched yellow buildings across from a trash-strewn, seriously neglected schoolyard (surrounding an equally abused elementary school building) where ten-year-olds raced around kicking under-inflated soccer balls on the sooty, crusted snow. An understated brass plaque next to the door identified the Press Center in both Russian and English.

I tugged open the heavy wooden door and then pushed the second, even heavier inner door into a small foyer. The aroma of fresh coffee wafted up to me as I stood there staring at the middle-aged woman with the no-nonsense gaze and henna-ed hair sitting behind the desk.

"My name is Michelle," I told her in Russian. "I work here."

The *dezhurnaya* gave me that wide-eyed, quizzical look I would come to know very well in the next few months, the look that asked what a middle-aged American woman with grown children was doing living alone in Moscow without her husband. Russians understand single women with children—in fact, there are as many divorces as marriages in Russia—but this woman had a husband whom she'd left half a world away to live in a country where one's family was the only support system society offered.

I didn't know then what a curiosity I would become. I was just happy to have "arrived."

My office wasn't much more than a closet at the top of the stairs on the second floor, but it had a tall, narrow double-casement window that looked across a driveway to another office building. The *fortochka* stood ready to open if I needed air.

What I needed most in my tiny office was heat. Apparently it once had been a large upstairs storeroom with no radiator of its own. The *dezhurnaya* found a portable heater (perched precariously on three of its four plastic legs) and brought it up to my office. If I put it behind my chair, it did a pretty good job of keeping me warm enough to work. (Translated, that means that my fingers weren't too stiff to type, and my breath wasn't visible in the frosty air when I answered the phone.)

That night I sent off another e-mail to Laurie describing the office:

> The walls are a pale urine yellow and the once-white
> curtains on the window are ripped in several places,
> but everything seems to be clean—no doubt thanks to
> Zhenya, the cleaning woman I met this morning. She

chattered away as soon as I introduced myself, and I
think she said she'd fix the curtains.

That's one of the problems of knowing not-quite-
enough Russian: I can ask questions, but I can't always
understand the answers. Or the other way around.

Just yesterday, I was casing the neighborhood around
my apartment in a rare burst of January sunshine,
peeking into the shops, studying the length of the
currency exchange lines, queuing up to buy a bottle of
red Georgian wine at the kiosk by the bus stop (cheap
at any price and not bad with pasta for dinner). I had
started back to my flat with the wine in my backpack
when a young woman carrying a child, maybe two years
old, rushed up to me. The child was having some sort of
seizure, and the young woman was frantic and exhausted
from running! "The hospital! Where's the hospital?"

I knew where it was, but to reply would have taken
too much time and she might not have understood
me. I scooped the little boy into my arms and hurried
down the street, through the driveway behind my
flat (taking care to stay in the middle where cars had
worn tracks for better footing). I headed across a dirt
path through the snow (created when parents piled up
fresh snow to make a sledding hill for the kids) to the
back door of the polyclinic on the next street over. I
shouted, in Russian, that we needed help (a phrase I'd
rehearsed often enough) and put the boy in the arms
of the doctor who turned around at the commotion.
The young woman, gasping and clutching her side,
trailed after the doctor.

I watched the automatic door close behind them,
paused long enough to catch my breath (and realize that
hospitals everywhere smell like Lysol and oil paint),
and headed home. This time I did understand what she
needed, and I really didn't need to reply. I never saw her
or the child again, but I felt as if I'd passed some kind of
test for a resident of Moscow.

In the office, I've got a red plastic rotary telephone that looks like one of those toy phones the kids loved. It's hard-wired into the wall. So much for the touch-tone phone with answering machine I brought from home! And that's about it for office equipment. Tomorrow Renny and I are going to buy my computer and printer (which the USIA grant pays for), and I guess we'll figure out a way to hook up the modem. I may have to run a phone wire into the next office where I saw a phone outlet like the one in my flat.

I've made one stab at decorating already. I pinned up that wall-sized map of the Soviet Union that I brought. I think it dates from 1977. Of course, all the city names are the Soviet ones, not the historic ones that are used again today, but I'll put pins in all the cities I visit. I already marked Moscow, Minsk, Gomel, Tallinn, Volgograd, and St. Petersburg—I gave myself credit for my earlier trips.

The best thing about the office is that it has a door I can close when a press conference is scheduled across the hall. Apparently, the hallway is the designated "smoking area," and you know how much I like that!

It's small but I have a *shkaf*—sort of a wall unit of cabinets—where I can hang up my coat and leave my boots and long underwear. Everyone goes through a ritual each morning, taking off all the outside layers and putting on indoor shoes and sweaters. Renny calls it his Mr. Rogers routine! I'm going to leave a pair of heels at work so I don't have to carry them back and forth every day.

So now, Honey, you should have visual pictures of the places where I spend most of my time. I'll take pictures and send them so you'll have an even better idea. Then you can imagine me sitting at my desk missing you.

LAURIE'S E-MAILS WERE usually comforting—full of the daily trivia of his work (on a contract to create a warehouse automation system), weekend repairs, laundry, his efforts to learn to cook, the cats, church, friends, and reports on Robyn and David. But one that arrived later in the month was anything but comforting.

"The project in Stockton is still hung up," he wrote. "The radio frequency signals still don't operate properly, and the vendor doesn't seem to have a solution. We just keep testing and training and retraining the forklift drivers, but it's getting me down. I know Del Monte expects this project to go online in March and right now I don't see how we'll make that window. Same old thing, but when I'm blue, I miss you more than ever."

I could feel the tension in his words, tension that I could sometimes dissolve with pillow talk about how much Del Monte needed him on this project and depended on him to install this system that used UPC codes and radio frequency signals into an AS400 computer. It would manage the inventory of Del Monte food products at the warehouse in Stockton in the San Joaquin Valley, about seventy miles east of San Mateo.

I sensed his doubts—most of them instilled three years before when he was manager of the data processing operations for Del Monte in the glass-and-steel skyscraper at the foot of the Bay Bridge in San Francisco. Del Monte announced that it was "outsourcing" its data processing division to EDS, the big DP conglomerate that Ross Perot founded years ago. It was going to be super smooth and painless, Laurie found himself explaining to his staff. All the employees would just become EDS employees at the same rate of pay and the same level of seniority. They would even stay in the same offices.

So, after twenty-five years with Del Monte, the only company he ever worked for after college, he threw himself completely into learning the EDS "way." He read the volumes of management skills that EDS required of their managers; he learned to repeat the mantra of "empowering" employees as the company's most valuable resource.

He was probably the most effective disciple of the new system— right up to the day six months later when a stranger walked into his office with cardboard boxes and told him EDS was restructuring its Del Monte operations and there was no place for him in the new arrangement. The stranger, known forever after as the Angel of Death, told him to be out of the building with all his personal belongings within an hour and, by the way, "please don't speak to anyone on your way out."

He was forty-eight years old and unemployed after twenty-six years of productive work, nearly all of that with a single company. It was a familiar tune that he'd heard lots of friends sing before, but nothing had prepared us for the impact it would have on him.

I was relaxing on the deck in the backyard of our hillside home when he came in that June day. I almost always got home before him since my office was a brief, seven-minute commute away. The day was very warm and I was sipping iced tea. He walked across the deck, sat down next to me, and put both his hands on my arm. He was trembling.

"What's the matter, honey?"

He started to speak and discovered he had almost no voice. His words were thready, distorted, and nearly impossible to hear. "I lost my job today."

He looked as if he'd been beaten. He flopped back in the deck chair and rested his head on his chest as he repeated the indignities of the day. I had the sense that he was completely emptied of life and vitality, only the outside shell was left. He wasn't angry, just hurt and feeling worthless and tossed aside.

"Honey, this isn't the worst thing in the world." I struggled to pour something real and living back into him. "So, you don't have a job. I have a job, and you'll find another one. You have incredibly marketable skills. It's their loss that they can't see what they have thrown away. They can't diminish you unless you let them.

"You are still the same wonderful, loving, supportive husband and father you were when you left this house this morning. Only now you have more free time! Now the only job you have is finding another one!"

It took seven exasperating and often depressing months of high anticipation and dashed hopes as one job possibility after another appeared, gained steam, and then evaporated. He was almost obsessive about finding another job soon. He worked into the early morning hours over his resume, his cold-call letters, his networking, and the Silicon Valley want ads. The only break he allowed himself was a daily noontime episode of *People's Court* on television.

He and another friend in the same situation even checked out those come-ons for small businesses like coin-operated laundromats and fast-food franchises. Most of the time he was able to laugh about them—at least I thought he was laughing.

Sometime later I was rummaging through some unlabeled audio cassettes stacked by the stereo in search of one piece of choral music. In frustration, I popped one cassette after another into the slot and then was stopped stock-still to hear Laurie's voice. It was a tape that an employment consultant had made as she and he role-played a job interview in the weeks just after he lost his job. His voice was nearly unrecognizable: quavering, high-pitched, and wispy. He was beaten.

For some irrational reason, he had always been insecure about his job skills. In the first letter I sent my parents after we settled in San Francisco, right after our wedding, I wrote, "Laurie's confidence is starting to build. He was worried that he hadn't learned enough in college and that Del Monte would realize they had made a mistake in hiring him. I think he knows better now."

But twenty-six years later, it was as if he felt that he had been conning them all that time, that he had finally been found out.

In the end, he found a job, but it was a bit like kissing his sister. He went back to Del Monte, but this time as a consultant to carry out the warehouse automation project he had begun before the outsourcing to EDS. The project went to EDS with Laurie and when EDS dumped him, Del Monte pulled the project back. They believed in Laurie and the project—as long as he was heading it up.

Del Monte wanted him at the helm but—so sorry—they were under a hiring freeze so would he do it as a contract employee at the same salary he had been making at EDS (but, of course, without benefits)?

My reaction to the offer was bittersweet. Laurie was so eager to be sought out, longing to be recognized for his abilities, that I knew he desperately wanted to take it. I, more than anything else, wanted those things for him, too. But I also could plainly see that Del Monte was using him.

I knew him. He would sacrifice himself to deliver this project— which in many ways was unique. It had never been done before, this way, by any other manufacturing company, and once Stockton was under way, Del Monte planned to replicate it in their warehouses across the country—no doubt with Laurie at the helm, and probably still with no permanent job or benefits.

But he was drawn to this project for another reason. It was designed to use those familiar bars and lines of the Universal Product Code to carry information from the warehouse pallet to the company computer by scanning wands installed on forklifts in the warehouses. Those UPC codes held special meaning for Laurie since he had led the team that wrote the first computer program that would place those carefully sequenced bars and lines on can labels. His program, written for Del Monte, was shared (sold?) throughout the industry, and UPC codes became the cornerstone of shopping, inventory, and warehousing that they are today.

So this project was an appropriate culmination of work he had started twenty years earlier at Del Monte.

But it was also a project that was grinding him up right now, and I wasn't there to cushion the blows or hold him when words didn't seem to work. His e-mail message hit me like a blow to the gut.

What did I think I was doing? Of course, he urged me to have my Great Adventure—for me, not for him. This was all for me, to challenge myself, to see if I could live alone in a foreign culture at age fifty and succeed, to see if I could grab the golden ring. What an incredible self-indulgence!

Now he needed me and I couldn't do anything but send sterile, electronic messages from a distance of ten thousand miles.

My homesickness was pretty rough that night. I cried myself to sleep and awoke in the morning to mascara smudges on the big, square European pillows and salty tear trails down my cheeks. My twenty-eighth wedding anniversary was coming up later that week, on January 28, and I knew I was on shaky ground. What a joke it would be if I didn't even make it through the month, let alone the year?

I had barely settled into my office that morning after doing my Mr. Rogers' Routine and fetching coffee from downstairs when the *dezhurnaya* burst in the door, shouting for me to come down. "A surprise! A surprise from California!"

Nearly everyone in the office was gathered around a young woman in a fur coat and hat who was holding an arrangement of roses up for everyone to admire. With great ceremony, she handed them to me. "From your husband! From America!"

Murmurs of oohs and aahs and then applause as I carried the flowers up to my office with everyone else trailing close behind. The roses weren't the big deal; roses can be purchased on street corners in most of the cities of Russia, even in the depths of winter. What was unique was the idea of "wiring" flowers from America for delivery in Moscow. I'm sure most of my co-workers thought these very rosebuds had been flown from California.

Russians are sentimental and romantic, and they appreciate those qualities in others. Americans don't have that reputation abroad so my officemates were pleasantly surprised and approving.

I tried to tell them it was for my anniversary, but I couldn't remember the word for it in Russian. I managed "day of my wedding," and the right words in Russian were passed around the crowd.

Through my tears I explained, in English now, that on my first anniversary Laurie had brought me a single red rose, then two for the second anniversary and so on. Then on our tenth anniversary, I was back to a single rose, a white one. I always thought it was perfect symmetry that my mathematician husband would develop a base-ten system for something as romantic as giving flowers to his wife.

In this arrangement, of course, were two white ones and eight red ones, representing twenty-eight years. One of the English speakers translated for the others.

I read the piece of teletype that was stapled to the card. "Happy Anniversary, Honey. The florist said I could wire these to Russia and I guess I did. I love you, Laurie."

Later in the day, when I returned to my office from lunch, I noticed that one of the red roses had been removed from the spray and tucked into a bud vase by itself. I understood the message.

In Russia, flowers for celebratory occasions are always given in odd-numbered groups; flowers in even-numbered groups are reserved for the dead, to be taken to funerals or grave sites. The only exception to that rule is when a husband gives an even-numbered bouquet to his wife: It means he wants a divorce!

Someone in my office had taken the time to make sure that Laurie's intention wasn't misunderstood.

Laurie's anniversary roses.

That night I wrapped that single red rose in plastic and then put it in the bottom of a canvas bag to keep it from freezing on my long trek back home. I tied the yellow ribbon from the arrangement around it and put it in a bud vase on the piano in my flat where it rested—dry and brittle—among the photographs of my family until I repacked my belongings one very short late fall day when it was time to go home.

BUT THE FLOWERS were still fresh when I entertained for the first time in Moscow. Oleg, who had been an interpreter on my first trip in 1988, and his wife Elena were coming to dinner now that my landlady had moved a very serviceable dining room table and chairs into the window end of my living room. We would celebrate the third birthday of their son Gleb!

Oleg and Elena would hate the label, but I saw them as pioneers of Russia's new middle class. They had a washing machine and a multi-format VCR and would have disposable diapers for their daughter, their *second* child, who would be born that summer. Their decision to have a second child, by itself, was enough to establish their new status, but their plans to buy a flat in Moscow after selling their tiny one-room apartment in a distant suburb confirmed it.

Three years ago Oleg was a linguistics professor, and Elena taught music in an elementary school. They could not have been more vulnerable when the economic revolution steamrolled this country. In the new Russia, teachers and scientists were on the bottom rung, rarely paid—and only a pittance when they were. They depended on their families to help them keep nutritious food on the table and to buy milk for Gleb.

Then they got a break. Through someone who knew someone, Oleg was hired by a western law firm as a translator/interpreter. He would be paid a reasonable wage and, even better, he would find himself in an environment where he could learn how to work this new system, legally and honestly, to benefit himself and his family.

He was a quick study. Now the law firm is sending him to law school (although he's also finishing up his Ph.D.) since they recognize the need to have Russian staffers who understand legal principles and Russian law (convoluted and arcane as it is). He's valued for his ability, and he's being paid accordingly.

What a concept!

Newspapers here are full of stories about the "new Russians" with their leather trench coats, BMWs, cell phones, and wads of cash they're hell-bent on spending. They're the ones buying gold-plated bathroom fixtures, vacationing in Russian enclaves in Spain, and building ostentatious, three-story *dachas* next to gingerbread cottages in the countryside.

Polite Russians call them entrepreneurs; others call them *mafia*, justifiably or not. An acquaintance in Vladivostok had another name for them when I asked who lived in those tacky monstrosities under construction at the edge of the city. Democrats! he snarled.

Whatever you call them, they represent one extreme in modern Russian society. The vast majority of Russians, unfortunately, make up the other extreme—the ones who are just barely getting by or those who've fallen through the net altogether.

But Oleg, Elena, and their (soon to be) two-child nuclear family fall comfortably in the middle. They don't have a car (or even a telephone since the central-planners didn't see the need for that service in their suburb), but they do have a snazzy collapsible buggy for the baby and Disney videos for their three-year-old.

Most of all they understand how the system can work for them.

They are the founding members of the middle class, the newest Russians of all. At the moment, it's still the smallest and most fragile group in Russian society, the group most in need of cultivation and nurturing. For if Russia is going to make it with a market economy (no doubt, one of its own, uniquely Russian design), then it will need a vital and flourishing middle class that is financially comfortable and relatively unworried about survival.

It will need a nation of Olegs and Elenas who worry about finding good schools for their children, health care for their parents and, perhaps, a flat in the city with a telephone, who are relaxed enough about their lives to exercise their citizenship and to demand decent behavior from the bureaucrats who serve them, who are prepared to carry the burden of nation-building on their shoulders.

Without a doubt, Oleg would laugh at those descriptions. He has no such inflated views of his role in the new Russia. But just last week I heard him debating the merits of mortgages (which wouldn't be available in Russia for some years to come) and complaining about office politics.

Sounded pretty middle class to me.

Letters From Russia
Now, about the locks

MOSCOW — After a couple of weeks in my flat on the embankment of the Moscow River, I finally met my neighbors—the hard way.

Although the doors to our apartments are less than five feet apart, we had never actually spoken to each other. We both had politely avoided opening our doors until the other had gotten on the lift or headed down the stairs. I knew from looking at the configuration of the windows on the outside wall of the building that they had a much larger flat but, other than that, all I knew was that my landlady said they were wonderful people.

I mostly thought of them as ghosts that I occasionally heard but never saw. That is, until I came home from work on a Monday afternoon, put the key in the lock and it wouldn't turn. I wrestled with the unyielding lock and key for fifteen minutes before I accepted the fact that I was in trouble. This was my worst fear come true. I needed help, and I didn't know a soul.

Of course, there really was no excuse for not having met my neighbors. No doubt, my mother would have been on intimate terms with everyone in the building by now. But this wasn't Smalltown USA; this was a city where people don't open their doors when they hear a scream for fear the attacker will turn on them, where people install triple dead-bolts on steel doors and buy German shepherds to snarl at strangers. And I was the strangest of strangers—a middle-aged American woman living alone in a city of more than ten million Russians.

So now what? I couldn't get into my super-secure flat, and I didn't have a clue how to call a locksmith or find a phone to call my landlady. I refused to allow myself to panic; I didn't leave home and family to come ten thousand miles around the globe to burst into tears the first time I got in a jam. Nonetheless, I couldn't for the life of me remember the Russian words to describe my situation, and my knees were decidedly wobbly.

The neighbors' doorbell was just a few feet from mine so I reached up and pushed it. The door was opened by a boy about ten, and I managed to explain who I was and why I needed help. Was his mother home? Yes, not only his mother, but his father and his brother, too—his nineteen-year-old brother who had just come back from spending a year studying in Vancouver, British Columbia, who spoke English!

Within minutes I was seated at the kitchen table while Mama made tea and Papa went to work on my door. The older son was rousted from his nap to help with interpretation, if needed.

I called my landlady who then discussed the situation with Mama, and it was decided to call a repairman. I mistakenly thought we were calling a locksmith. However, in just a few minutes, the repairman was trying to turn the key with no more success than I had had. He then said he would have to get his instruments. I had visions of lock-picks.

Wrong!

He returned with a crowbar, sledgehammer, and other similarly delicate "instruments."

While I drank tea and showed photos of my family to Mama, the hallway echoed with the clangs of metal-on-metal. In thirty minutes or so, Papa returned to say the door was open. I cringed to think of what was left. Amazingly, there still was a door and most of the frame. Enough so that I could still use the simple lock in the doorhandle.

The repairman left after promising to return the next day with a new dead-bolt. Then the neighbors all came into my flat and helped me clean up the mess. Papa brought over a steel bar that worked rather like The Club car lock and showed me how to brace it against the door when I went to bed. I declined their invitation to supper but not their offer to keep an eye on my flat while I was at work the next day. Mama said she would be home all day.

When I closed the door and heard them close theirs, I relaxed for the first time in hours. I knew my neighbors now—and, just as my landlady said—they were wonderful people.

Chapter Four

MY PERIOD OF settling in, nesting at home and at the office, was over. It was time to take my show on the road, time to see how receptive newspaper editors in the regions would be to the suggestions of this American newspaper editor about newsroom management and newspaper design.

The collapse of the Soviet Union four years earlier had turned the newspaper industry in Russia on its ear. Throughout the Soviet period, newspapers in the western sense didn't exist, replaced by government organs that printed largely what they were told to print. They were the ultimate "gray ladies." Now, if they were to survive, they had to recreate themselves as a pleasing visual and information product that people actually wanted to buy. They had to compete for business at the same time they were learning how to gather and report legitimate news and (gasp!) sell advertising.

The result, as with so many issues in a new democratic Russia, was generational. The stolid, dull-eyed editors of the Soviet period resisted this dramatic shift with every fiber of their being; the kids in their newsrooms ate it up. They were the ones who had been stopping by the library at RAPIC to ask for books on newspaper design since nothing on the subject was available in Russian.

Russia has a long history of appreciation for art and design. I've spent long hours at the Russian Museum in St. Petersburg admiring the incredible fifteenth century iconography of Andrei Rublev, the portraits of Vladimir Borovikovsky from the 1800s or avant-garde art of Malevitch and Kandinsky. During the Soviet period, modernists were producing remarkable work, and even state-sponsored propagandists turned out eye-popping examples of gigantism and brutalism on posters and billboards and in sculpture.

Designers didn't have to look far for inspiration, but few of them thought of newsprint as a proper medium. With few exceptions, Russian newspapers remained dull and dry, and the young page designers with flair were reined in at every turn. I thought I might offer a boost to those kids who dared to be bold.

When I e-mailed the RAPIC director last fall to ask about developing a program for my USIA assignment, I suggested newspaper design—something I had a fair amount of experience with—and he jumped at the possibility. Two of those fifteen boxes that I hauled through Customs at the airport were filled with manuals and Society of Newspaper Design yearbooks brimful of examples of good design from around the world. As soon as my computer system was up and running, I started preparing the outline of a three-hour seminar that would launch my program for newspaper editors outside of Moscow.

I'd done a couple of trial runs for journalism students in Moscow, but everyone said not to bother with Moscow editors. They were too sophisticated to listen to all the American consultants who were popping in and out of Russia. I'd have plenty of time for them later—if they cared to listen.

I was also warned about the serious handicap I brought with me— my gender! As a rule, Russian men aren't particularly interested in taking direction from any woman, and nearly all Russian editors were men. My stuff would have to be especially juicy to turn their heads.

So, I looked to the RAPIC staff for advice, in particular to Vladimir Svetozarov, my dear Svet—tall, courtly, and extremely proper with this American woman, just about his age, who had been dropped at his doorstep.

Where should I go for the first seminar?

To St. Petersburg, of course!

We talked at his desk in a crowded corner of an office he shared with his assistant, the fax machine, and the office mailboxes. He didn't seem to notice the commotion around him, but he was a bit nervous with me. He stroked his neat gray mustache and ran his hands through his full head of bristly iron-gray hair.

I must go to Anna Sharogradskaya, the director of the RAPIC office in St. Petersburg. She would take care of everything. No argument from me! Ever since my first trip in 1988, I had been looking for the chance to go back.

He jumped up and squinted at his wall-size day organizer above his desk. He stabbed at the first Monday in February. Okay? We would see how many editors Anna could get, "probably just a few since it's St. Petersburg and they're sophisticated there too."

Svetazarov was a newspaperman of the first order. He had served for years as the chief of bureau for the Russian News Agency TASS in Tehran. He spoke Farsi as well as excellent, very formal English (and a smattering of German, French, and Arabic). He had a good understanding of the free press/free speech issues that most of the visiting USIA journalists came to discuss—and an equally cynical view of the value of their opinions. After moderating a seminar that featured an American newspaper publisher, talking at length about First Amendment protections, he muttered to an associate within my earshot, "Give them something they can actually use."

I didn't think much of those lectures either, and I was determined that my seminars would be full of practical advice, tips, and hints for producing reader-friendly newspapers that could survive in the cut-throat economic market that was emerging in Russia. There were too many newspapers—as many as twenty in some medium-sized cities. Most were going to have to die for the strongest to survive; perhaps I could help a few editors to be among those standing at the end.

Svet really didn't know what to make of me, but he would do the best he could. He would send me out under the wing of Anna Sharogradskaya, who, I quickly learned, was legendary for her tender care and feeding of visiting journalists.

"Oh, St. Petersburg! Anna will take care of you!" I heard over and over as I discussed the trip with co-workers. It sounded great to me. I was prepared to be brave and courageous and all that, but I would never turn my back on a healthy dose of TLC when it was offered.

As it turned out I wouldn't even have to make the overnight train trip by myself. Paul Janensch, the former editor of the *Louisville Courier-Journal*, was in Moscow working on a grant to set up partnerships between Russian and American newspapers. He needed to make contacts in St. Petersburg so he and his Russian assistant Lusya would come along too.

AT LENINGRADSKIY VOKZAL (train station), we joined a group huddled outside one of the first-class *vagoni* (cars) and began stomping our feet to maintain some feeling in them while we waited.

We could see the attendant standing just inside the door, watching us watching her as we shivered in the bitter, wind-whipped cold. The mutual staring went on until ten minutes before the train was to depart when she finally flung open the door and lowered the steps to let us board.

She took our tickets, handed them back and said, "Wrong train. Your train is on the next platform."

Whoa! We had a whopping seven minutes to run (on the ice!) the length of the platform, around the front of the next train and down to the right car to board. We made it, panting and perspiring, just as the conductor in that car was about to pull up the steps.

While we were still struggling to get our bags down the narrow aisle to our compartment, our train started moving away from the station. That was my very real introduction to the fact that, in Russia, the trains run on time, exactly on time, and sometimes they are less than ten minutes apart to the same destination.

I collapsed in nervous laughter on one of the bench seats in the compartment as Paul and Lusya settled in across from me. I'm sure Lusya was embarrassed by these bumbling Yanks in her company, but Paul and I were determined to have a great time.

After all, we were off to Russia's cultural capital, the city Peter the Great carved out of the delta lowland where the Neva River spilled into the Gulf of Finland and then the Baltic Sea. In the first decade of the eighteenth century, seafaring and maritime trade captured the imagination of the young tsar. He needed an ice-free port to follow those dreams so he conscripted serfs from all over European Russia to drain the swamps and build a city of his design. The Peter and Paul Fortress, which still stands with its iconic obelisk, was the first fire-resistant stone building of the young city, and in 1712, Peter moved the seat of government from Moscow to St. Petersburg, his Window on the West.

Built along the Neva River and dozens of granite-banked canals, the city of eight hundred bridges is lined with brilliantly colored palaces that look more Italian Renaissance than Russian. The most recognizable of them all is the massive green and white Winter Palace, the official residence of the Romanovs and, of course, the seminal image of the Revolution of 1917. Today it houses the spectacular Hermitage Art Museum which showcases the European masters (and all the French Impressionists the Louvre turned up its nose at).

We were finally starting to relax, allowing the rocking of the train and the *shampanskoye* we'd brought along, to lull us toward sleep, when Paul happened to drop his visa out of his passport. I picked it up.

"Paul, you look like a terrorist, a smiling, blond terrorist!" I started to hand it back but something caught my eye.

"Did you know that your visa's expired?"

Those are scary words for a foreigner living in Russia. You could be required to present your passport and visa any time you came up against some form of Russian officialdom—or if officialdom chose to come up against you. You needed a passport and valid visa to exchange money, to pick up a package at the post office, to check into a hotel—as we were planning to do the next morning in St. Petersburg.

It couldn't be, he shot back. However, he couldn't read Russian so he passed it to Lusya. She nodded. It had expired on February 1.

Paul, usually urbane and witty, had a pretty short fuse. He exploded in a fury of accusations about the idiots who had arranged his travel documents and at his own failure to get everything checked for himself. Then he calmed down just as quickly. Maybe it could be extended in St. Petersburg.

Maybe, but we might as well get some sleep. We couldn't do anything about it on the train.

With that, Lusya and I made up our bunks, and Paul moved to the next compartment where he would share a cabin with a Russian businessman he'd never met before. As usual, I fell asleep immediately. Rocking trains were like cradles for me.

It was still quite dark when we pulled into the Moskovskiy Vokzal in St. Petersburg and Anna Sharogradskaya, a fifty-ish bundle of fur and leather with owlish horn-rimmed glasses and a very un-Russian uncovered head, was waiting with carnations and motherly embraces. She proved to be as unflappable as everyone had promised.

No visa? She shrugged when we spilled our tale of woe. No one knows. They might not even notice. And if they do, well then, we'll do something else.

With her handbag under her arm and short black hair whipping in the wind, she charged off. We bobbed like serfs in her wake.

But they did notice. The director of the service bureau at the Oktyabrskaya Hotel announced loudly to anyone who cared to listen that no one without the proper documents would stay at her hotel.

"Send them to the Europeyskaya (the three-hundred-dollar-a-night palace in the center of town). They won't care," she wailed with indignation. "But without documents in order, they won't stay at the Oktyabrskaya."

And we didn't. At least Paul and I didn't. Lusya got her room and I probably could have gotten one—although I didn't have St. Petersburg listed on my visa—except for Paul's much more serious transgression.

Not to worry, Anna cooed, as she herded us to the RAPIC office in the *Dom zhurnalista* (House of Journalists) on Nevskiy Prospekt and plied us with tea and biscuits. The Europeyskaya wasn't an option on our budget, but she would find something. She would just make some phone calls.

"Something" did turn up some time after dinner and, since taxis still hadn't taken hold in St. Petersburg, Anna flagged a car and negotiated with the driver to take us. Once in the car, Anna whispered in my ear, Are you brave?

What could I say? Of course!

We rode on in silence as I imagined what lay ahead. We knew that she was taking us to a flat, owned by a friend, that was awaiting *remont* (repair). The friend had managed to buy the flat a couple of years earlier when private ownership became possible, but she couldn't afford a *remont*. I wasn't surprised, and I remembered thinking, how bad could it be?

The driver stopped at an archway on a quiet side street, and Anna led us over and around the piles of soot-encrusted snow and through the icy courtyard to a nondescript entryway with a keyless lock. Anna punched in the code as Paul and I read it to her from a scribbled note by the light of a match, and we walked into the now-expected pitch-dark hallway and felt our way up the first flight of concrete stairs to the second-floor landing. I nearly gagged at the stench of urine.

Anna found a light switch and unlocked the heavy metal door of flat No. 5, pulled it open, and then tackled the two locks on the inner door. I was scarcely breathing, but Paul hadn't heard the "Are you brave?" conversation; he was just tired. The visa business had sapped his energy.

The inner door swung open, and we stepped into another world.

The flat was enormous with twelve- or fifteen-foot high walls and remnants of elaborately carved molding. The ceilings had once been magnificent with rococo *bas relief* remaining in some of the rooms.

The front rooms faced the street along a canal. Small sitting rooms canted out over the sidewalk with tall, double-casement windows on three sides. They opened from the central hall with huge, richly carved double doors that had been painted over with whitewash.

Bare light bulbs hung where cut crystal chandeliers had once been, and paint peeled from what may have been silver sconces on the walls. Seriously worn Oriental carpets covered the over-scrubbed and splintered remains of hardwood parquet floors.

Everything was clean, but the sour, musty smell of mold permeated the flat, which had obviously been recently overheated for our welcome. Large portions were rather primitively boarded up so we had to wend our way around the lean-to in the middle to see the open rooms.

I was sure we were about to occupy one floor of one of St. Petersburg's eighteenth century mansions, now gone to seed, when I ventured into the kitchen where five small gas stoves and four tiny refrigerators lined the walls. Water dripped from the tap into the one overburdened sink.

Paul was standing in the middle of the room. Why all the stoves and refrigerators?

It must have been a communal flat, I offered.

"Yes, five or six families, maybe even ten, lived here at one time," Anna said in a flat, distant whisper. "The rooms would have been divided by curtains. There was no privacy, no secrets. You never knew who was listening."

Hollywood's interpretation of the post-1917 Moscow mansion of *Dr. Zhivago* flashed across my mind. I tried to push it away since I knew that Russians considered the movie made from Boris Pasternak's *samizdat* (underground) novel nothing more than laughable because of the careless attempt to recreate a Russian landscape in Spain. The misspelled street signs and banners spoiled an otherwise marvelous movie.

Actually, calling up some of poetry of Anna Akhmatova (perhaps *Requiem*, her indictment of Stalinist terror) or Mikhail Bulgakov's anti-Soviet farce *The Master and Margarita* would have shaped a more truthful picture, but that Zhivago mansion with the tattered velvet drapes hung as room dividers stayed with me as I poked around.

The bathroom was a disaster, but the toilet did flush. Clean towels and linens were laid out, and someone had stocked one of the refrigerators with sausage, cheese, eggs, and milk. Fresh bread, bottles of mineral water, and a box of tea sat on the table. Over-stuffed sofas in the two sitting rooms that fronted one of the canals had been pulled out flat and made up as beds.

Anna, it's absolutely fine, I told her, and, of course, it was. We had everything we needed, and nothing in this museum of Russia's past required any degree of bravery on our part.

"Draw us a map so we can get to *Dom zhurnalista* (House of Journalists) in the morning, and thank you for working whatever magic you did to find us this place."

After we had our map and several lessons in unlocking and lock-ing the doors, she left. Paul and I looked at each other and burst out laughing. I claimed the room with a *fortochka* that actually opened and unpacked my bag.

WHEN WE ARRIVED at Anna's office the next morning, several editors from newspapers in and around St. Petersburg had already begun to arrive. The *samovar* was heating water for tea as they unbundled themselves from their heavy coats and fur hats and settled around the U-shaped conference table in the adjoining library.

Unlike a group of editors from any single region in the U.S., they didn't talk to each other—no kibitzing over the day's news or the price of newsprint or the latest press law. They sat quietly with their pens and notebooks at the ready; the only conversation was between colleagues from the same paper.

This curious scene would repeat itself over and over as I took my dog-and-pony show across the eleven times zones of this enormous country. Editors and journalists in Russia didn't seem to share the commonality of purpose that those in the U.S. did. They were suspicious of each other, as if they were afraid they would spill some sensitive trade secret to a competitor.

It wouldn't take me long to conclude that this lack of conviviality in a professional setting constituted one of the main barriers to forming regional professional associations that would promote the newspaper industry, provide professional training, share ideas and problem-solving, and lobby the newly formed democratic institutions for workable press laws.

It was all the more curious because I knew that these same people could have a terrific time together once the professional activities had been disposed of and the vodka and champagne came out.

But the people sitting in front of me that February morning were prepared to hear a lecture from a visiting American "expert." A lecture, however, was the furthest thing from my mind. We'd have a dialogue—and if they wouldn't participate, I'd badger them until they did.

I had carefully rehearsed my introductory remarks in Russian:

"Menya zavoot Michelle Carter," I began.

My name is Michelle Carter. Until this year I was the chief editor of *The San Mateo Times,* a daily newspaper. The city of San Mateo is located thirty-three kilometers south of San Francisco in California near the Pacific Ocean.

The circulation of my newspaper is forty-five thousand, with about thirty-six pages every day, more on Saturday. We publish four editions every day. I have an editorial staff of about forty-five people, including reporters, editors, photographers, librarians, and clerks.

I want you to ask questions when they pop into your head; don't save them until I ask for them. I also want you to argue with me, challenge me. We will have a conversation, not a lecture, and you must do your part.

First, I need to know some things about you. Please tell me your name and title, the name of your newspaper, its circulation, how many days a week that you publish. So, please, will you begin?

And so they did. Slowly I learned a bit about the papers represented at that first seminar, and the twelve participants learned something about me. While they seemed to like the chance to tell something about themselves and their newspapers—and some chose to tell me a lot more than I had asked—they still weren't going to ask any uninvited questions.

About half an hour into the presentation, after the third or fourth time I'd asked if anyone had any questions with no response, I stopped.

"This is quite amazing. It appears that you agree with everything I've said, with every idea I've presented. No one has a single contrary thought."

The word "contrary" created something of a problem for the young interpreter who hesitated. He said he thought it would be impolite for the participants to challenge me, to argue, to offer differing ideas. He would proceed only after I had made it clear to him that contrary thoughts would generate a real conversation. It wasn't the Russian way of doing things, but if that was truly what I wanted.

And, finally, a breakthrough. A serious young man who had set a tape recorder in front of me when we began raised his hand.

"I think that your information about the use of serif and sans-serif fonts may be accurate for English, but I don't think it is true when you are using Cyrillic characters as we are."

Luckily I had some statistics from readership surveys done in Russia to back up my point that serif typefaces are more easily and quickly read and understood in text—even in Cyrillic, but I conceded the possibility that it was less important in Russia than in countries where Latin characters were used.

"But let's look at some of your newspapers and see how readable the text fonts really are."

I spread out several copies of the papers that Anna had assembled for me and motioned for the editors to gather round me at the front of the table. Very slowly, and one at a time, they came up and started pulling their papers out of the stack. That was the significant moment, the thaw.

From that time on, nearly every point I made was met by an observation or a comment.

- I think it would be dull to have all the text look the same.
- There's no room in our newspapers for photos. We can fill it up many times over with just words.
- It has been our tradition to tell readers what they should want, not for them to tell us.

To this day, Anna has a snapshot on the bulletin board in her office that tells the story of that first seminar in just one image. I was talking about cropping photographs dramatically and effectively, and I had turned to the interpreter, a very earnest young man named Alexei, as my example.

"Photographs do one of three things. They show action, convey emotion, or they identify. The best ones do all three at once.

"If emotion is what you want to show with the photograph, remember that emotion in the face is revealed in the eyes or the mouth," I said as I pointed to Alexei's eyes and mouth.

"Not in the ears—so crop them off if you don't need them," and I covered his ears with my hands. At that moment, Anna snapped the photo and caught Alexei with an unforgettable expression of shock and wonder.

THE FOUR SEMINARS in St. Petersburg were hugely successful, but our stay there wasn't all work. Anna had seen to that with a serious dose of St. Petersburg's unflagging culture.

She started with tickets to see the most exquisite production of the ballet *Giselle* that I'd ever seen. It was staged by the Kirov ballet company which had recently taken back its pre-revolutionary name, the Mariinskiy. The ballerina, who danced the title role, was so frail and childlike it was possible to accept the notion that she died of a broken heart.

After the next night's five-hour presentation of the folk opera *Ruslan and Lyudmila* at the equally lovely Maliy ("little") Theatre, Paul and I were ready to beg off a third night at the theater when Anna promised something very special.

"The press officer of the St. Petersburg administration called today with a surprise for you."

I knew very well that surprises were rare in Anna's world. I was quite sure she had pulled out every stop to produce this "surprise" if she had to enlist the help of the mayor's office. We should be ready at six thirty, Anna said, for our escort to take us to the benefit concert of world-renowned cellist Mstislav Rostropovich.

Ever since we arrived, St. Petersburg had been buzzing about this performance at Shostakovich Concert Hall where Rostropovich hadn't performed since he went into exile! One of Russia's own sons, who had snubbed the Soviets and made his home in the U.S. for the past twenty years, had come back to give a solo concert to benefit Pushkin House in St. Petersburg, a museum honoring writers and artists in this seat of Russian culture.

His performance at Shostakovich Hall was a story in itself. The cellist had been a student at Moscow Conservatory in 1948 when Shostakovich, who was one of his teachers, lost favor with Stalin and was forced to resign. Rostopovich dropped out of the conservatory in a loud and public protest. Years of harassment by the Soviet regime followed, and it came to a tipping point when he welcomed the outlawed writer Alexander Solzhenitsyn into his own home. All performing opportunities for the cellist and his wife, a celebrated soprano, dried up, and they left the USSR for good. In retaliation, the Soviets rescinded his citizenship.

But tonight the beloved Slava would return to a democratic Russia to play in Shostakovich Hall. This we could not miss.

Paul and I, herded by our very serious and non-English speaking host, Arkady, had to pass through three police cordons outside the concert hall. For nearly a quarter mile around the hall, Petersburg citizens were crowded in a wind-driven snowfall in hopes of getting one of the standing room spots on the second-floor mezzanine that circled the orchestra *partier* (section) on the main floor.

At one point, Arkady's effort to squeeze us through the throng was stymied, and I was pushed against the outside wall of the hall. I reached up to brace myself and my fingers caught the sharp edge of a bronze plaque. The light from the street lamp was dim but it was enough for me to read the message:

In this hall on September 25, 1941, during the Siege of Leningrad, the composer Dmitriy Shostakovich introduced his Seventh Symphony which became known as the Leningrad Symphony. It was performed by the Academic Symphony Orchestra in this, the Grand Hall of the Leningrad Philharmonic.

Ever after, it would be known as Shostakovich Hall in memory of the bespectacled young composer-turned-fireman who wrote the first two movements of the symphony at the Leningrad Conservatory during breaks from his responsibilities in the civilian Emergency Volunteer Corps. Those movements were broadcast across the Soviet Union on September 17 with Shostakovich himself giving this introduction:

"I speak to you from Leningrad at a time when brutal battle rages at its very gates . . . Two hours ago I finished the first two movements of a symphonic work . . . Why do I announce this? I announce this so that those listening to me now may know that life in our city goes on as usual."

Of course, those words were part of a *scripted* propaganda blitz that the young composer was caught up in but, at the time, they were just the ticket to lift the sagging morale of a nation mired in a world war that would cost them an entire generation of young men.

September 25 was chosen for the first concert hall performance because it was Shostakovich's birthday. The completed work, with two additional movements, premiered in Kuybyshev (now called Samara) to which the young fireman had been evacuated in the fall of 1941. Few music critics consider Shostakovich's *Symphony No. 7* to be his best but it had been nothing less than magical for the people of Leningrad who were caught in one of history's most dramatic struggles—the siege of nine hundred days that starved a quarter of the people in the city to death.

Finally, a path opened through the crowd, and we elbowed our way to the coatroom where we traded our outer garments for *nomerki* (numbered chits) and then plunged in again to make our way up the broad staircase to the main hall. Arkady then led us down to the fourth row where we could very nearly touch the spare, ladder-backed chair where Rostropovich would sit to perform.

The beauty of the hall was in its understatement. The walls were jade green and everything else was pure white, the moldings, the mezzanine railings, the carved backdrop of the stage. The only glitter came from crystal chandeliers that made the white all the more dazzling.

Arkady pointed out special features of the hall and people in the audience, and I gave Paul the gist of the conversation. Our host had pared his sentences down to the basics, and I was keeping up fairly well. He noted that most of the people filling the mezzanine were children. "Their instrument was their ticket. They brought their violins, their flutes, and they could come in and watch the maestro."

I worried about the children who were studying piano but my Russian wasn't up to being flippant.

After a string of official introductions that welcomed "our dear, dear Slava" back to Petersburg, Rostropovich himself appeared carrying his cello and accompanied only by a pianist who would join him on about half his selections. He looked vigorous and even playful as he tossed his shock of white hair back from his ruddy, round face.

He played magnificently, emotionally, even ardently—and we were close enough to watch the perspiration run down his face and catch an occasional droplet when he shook his head.

Although he played for more than ninety minutes, it was not enough for the crowd. With the staccato, rhythmic clapping Russians use to show appreciation, they brought Rostropovich back for two encores and then, finally, he was done.

But the celebration was just beginning. Slava picked his way through the carpet of flowers on the stage and spoke passionately about St. Petersburg, his music, this concert hall, and his life for more than half an hour. I glanced at Arkady and tears were spilling down his cheeks. Unselfconsciously he repeated again and again, "*Belikiy chelovek* (a great man). A great son of Russia!"

YEARS LATER, PAUL told me about an encounter he and Lusya had during this visit that didn't seem particularly significant at the time. They had expected to talk with St. Petersburg Mayor

Anatoly Sobchak, a powerful political figure in Russia at the time, about Paul's program in Russia, but instead they were greeted by "a balding, short, trim man, wearing a gray suit free of wrinkles, a white shirt, and a plain dark tie."

As Paul told the tale later, "The man listened to Lusya's translation of what I was saying but did not take his penetrating gray eyes off my face. He didn't ask any questions or interrupt me. He hardly moved. He showed no emotion. He neither smiled nor frowned. When I was finished, he stood, nodded, shook my hand firmly, turned around, and walked out of the room.

"Who was that?" Paul asked Lusya." "Oh, that was just the deputy mayor. He said his name is Vladimir Putin."

Five years later, President Boris Yeltsin shocked the world by resigning and naming Putin as his successor. Paul recalled the announcement on CNN. "Onto the stage strode a balding, short, trim man in a wrinkle-free gray suit. It was the former deputy mayor of St. Petersburg. A correspondent noted that Putin had been an agent in the KGB, the Soviet Union's secret police."

In 2001, President George W. Bush met with Putin in Slovenia and told reporters. "I looked the man in the eye. I found him to be very straightforward and trustworthy, and we had a very good dialogue. I was able to get a sense of his soul."

"I looked Putin in the eye too, but I didn't get a sense of his soul," Paul said later. "All I saw was a blank wall."

Letters From Russia
Peter the Great's Window to the West

ST. PETERSBURG — Just two years after reclaiming its name, there's little in St. Petersburg that feels like Leningrad any more.

Peter the Great began the construction of this city on the Baltic in the Eighteenth Century as his window to the West. Now, after a seventy-year interruption that Peter could never have envisioned, it's serving that same purpose again.

Even in a hard February freeze, St. Petersburg has a gloss that a difficult, even torturous, history hasn't been able to dull. The most extraordinary polished granite bridges arch over the Neva River as dozens of fat mallards sit on the ice below waiting to be fed. Artfully dressed shop windows along Nevskiy Prospekt tease shoppers as they do in Berlin or London or San Francisco.

Real taxis shuttle elegant women in furs. Traffic policemen on foot whistle down cars whose drivers actually stop and pay for their infractions on the spot. Conversations in English, French and Japanese are heard nearly as often as those in Russian.

While Moscow has plunged into *biznes* with a gritty vengeance, St. Petersburg seems to have sniffed out the best and shrugged off the worst—much as it did with communism. Even in the darkest days of Stalin, this city kept its past (and its future) in style. The gilt in the palaces of this city must have exhausted gold mines throughout Siberia, and those palaces survived—eluding the musty fate of most relics of the tsars in this country.

But, then, this is the city of the brilliant green and white Winter Palace with its Hermitage next door. Basking in the opulence of the museum's grand foyer, I recall my favorite story of Leningrad's Siege of Nine Hundred Days during World War II:

As the Germans approached the city in 1941, the art treasures of the Hermitage were crated and packed on train cars. Fourteen trains got out; the fifteenth did not. Those paintings were returned to the museum and buried in sand in the wine cellars of the Winter

Palace. The curator of the Hermitage and his staff moved into the museum to try to survive as six hundred thousand people starved to death in the city around them. But for nearly every one of those nine hundred days, the curator led a tour of the museum for anyone or no one and described in great detail the paintings that once hung over the blank, unfaded rectangles on the walls. Most non-combatants were evacuated after the terrible winter of 1941-1942, but the curator stayed and died there in the Hermitage near the end of the siege.

That same passion for culture still permeates this city. SRO crowds, including young children, pack the Mariinskiy Theater and the concert halls virtually every night.

Since I didn't have the budget for the pricey rooms of the Hotel Europa, I ended up "camping" in the mildewed, peeling, nearly empty rooms of one of St. Petersburg's mansions that hadn't escaped Stalin's heavy hand. This one, with twelve-foot ceilings and leaded bay windows, had been carved into communal apartments with single kitchens and leaky baths for as many families as could fit.

This apartment is vacant now, awaiting *remont,* the renovations that will put the egg back together again in a style befitting the elegance of this once—and future—Window to the West.

Chapter Five

"THE PLEASURE OF your company is requested at dinner at 7 p.m. Thursday at Spaso House, the residence of Ambassador and Mrs. Thomas Pickering." The great seal of the United States of America was at the top but it looked odd on the blurry fax paper copy in my hand.

I was just getting used to the idea that in this country mail was an iffy thing. Almost everything important was hand-delivered or faxed. More times than I care to remember I would wait on the train level in a Metro station where an acquaintance would step off a train, hand me an envelope or a packet, and then cross the platform and jump on the train heading back in the other direction. The station was usually a half-way point between us or a station that one of us would pass through during the day. Everyone who lived in Moscow transacted business this way; no one would have considered dropping that envelope or packet in the mail for a trip across the city. No one believed it would ever get there.

So I first learned of my invitation to dine with Ambassador and Mrs. Thomas Pickering by a fax which was unceremoniously stuffed in my Press Center mail box by the *dezhurnaya* who was clearly unimpressed by the great seal of the United States of America—or who didn't even recognize it. A full day later a linen paper and gold leaf version was hand delivered to the office but by then my surprise at the invitation had evolved into pure delight.

Not that most of the five thousand or so Americans living in this teeming city of more than ten million hadn't had an opportunity to visit Spaso House. But most had been there at one of the public events when they responded to an invitation published in the *Moscow Times* or the *Moscow Tribune*, the two English-language dailies in the city.

This was different—a private dinner, I would learn when I called the social secretary to RSVP, to celebrate the arrival in Moscow of the new ambassador from Spain.

I had a pretty strong inkling why I had been singled out for such an honor. An old friend of Ambassador Pickering was Tom Lantos, the congressman from my district in California whom I'd gotten to know very well in my role as the hometown newspaper editor. Lantos had taken a personal interest in my Children of Chernobyl project, inviting me to join a panel testifying before a Congressional committee in Washington about compromised life in Belarus, a land poisoned by Chernobyl's radioactive fallout.

Before I left for Russia this time, Lantos invited me to lunch with his wife Annette and, after some chit-chat, he pulled a thick packet in a bulging manila envelope from his briefcase. He had a favor to ask. While I was in Moscow as a Professional-in-Residence (PIR in government parlance), could I find out anything about the fate of Raoul Wallenberg, the Swedish diplomat in Budapest who used his official visa-issuing powers to save thousands of Hungarian Jews from the Holocaust? He wanted me, as a journalist with no links to the government, to see if I could find anything more, now that secret Cold War archives were cracking open in Russia's new era of *glasnost* (political transparency).

Lantos was one of those Hungarian Jews. Born in Budapest, he was sixteen when he was arrested and shipped off to a Nazi labor camp. He escaped twice, succeeded in his second attempt and found his way into the Hungarian resistance. His Aryan looks (blue eyes and blond hair) allowed him to move unchallenged around occupied Budapest. During one close escape, he found sanctuary in a safe house that Wallenberg maintained.

A few months before Victory Day, Wallenberg was arrested by the Red Army as an American spy (no matter that the U.S.S.R. and the U.S. were allies at the time), and the rest of his story is anybody's guess. The Soviets reported that he died at the famously brutal Lubyanka Prison in Moscow at the hands of the vicious KGB secret police—twice—once in 1947 and again in 1957. But dozens of independent sightings indicate he may have been alive as late as 1985.

Lantos seemed consumed by his debt to Wallenberg. As a congressman, he sponsored a bill to make him an honorary U.S. citizen, and I later learned that he had funded search efforts out of his own pocket. Just see if reporters in Moscow know anything about this, if anyone knows anywhere else to look, he asked. That's all.

I took the fat packet and felt like Atlas shouldering the weight of the world. I knew how to ask hard questions and duck when the flak flew, but was I up to this?

No doubt Lantos had sent a message to Pickering to "extend courtesies" to this particular constituent who was living alone in Moscow. Well, I'd take my "courtesies" however I got them, and this one held real promise.

But first there were logistics to work out. I couldn't just call a cab to pick me up at my doorstep and deliver me to Spaso House. First, I didn't actually know where Spaso House was and, second, Moscow had no cabs. Anyone who needed a ride just stepped to the curb facing oncoming traffic and extended his or her right hand out at about a 45-degree angle to the body and waited for a car—any car— to stop. It usually didn't take long since most drivers in Moscow were eager to pick up a few thousand extra rubles. Once the car stopped and a fare was negotiated, you got in and took off, hoping the driver was honest and knew his way around Moscow—a highly efficient system long before the Ubers and Lyfts of today's Shared Economy.

My Russian friends had warned me never to flag a car this way because I might be mugged or kidnapped or worse, but I did it any time I needed to get somewhere faster than I expected the buses or Metro to carry me. And it always worked. I put their well-meant advice in the same category as the warnings never to stand next to a clean car (since "those are the ones that get blown up!") or never to walk across the Borodinsky Bridge alone — great advice that I had to ignore if I expected to actually *live* in Moscow.

So the day before the dinner party, I asked for directions to the ambassador's residence (as any good Muscovite would do) and found, to my delight, that it was just off Stariy Arbat (Old Arbat Street). I probably passed within a hundred yards of it on my way to and from work every day. Next, I actually walked from my flat to Spaso House to time how long it would take me to get there on foot—about twenty minutes.

On the day of the party, I left work early, soaked for a while in my super-deep tub, and then took my time dressing up for the first time since I'd arrived. However, my plans had a few unresolved snags. I had to wear my boots to negotiate my way over the icy streets so I would have to carry my dressy heels in my ever-present "perhaps" bag just like every other Russian woman. ("Perhaps" we would find something to buy!) So another Mr. Rogers act would be required when I arrived.

I probably should have pulled wool tights on under my cocktail dress as well since a crust of ice was forming over the river but I just couldn't bear the thought of standing in the vestibule of the ambassador's home pulling off my tights. I could take the cold for twenty minutes for a party like this.

Finally there was the issue of the hat: If I wore my wool hat (which I surely would need), I would arrive with my hair plastered to my head—definitely not the image I had in mind after I had taken special pains with my "do." I compromised with Bette's silk shawl which I spread loosely over my head and tossed the ends over my shoulders. It wouldn't provide the warmth of the wool hat with the turned-up brim (which made me look a bit like Paddington Bear) but it would protect me from the biting Siberian wind that was picking up strength outside.

I really don't remember much about the walk, but I will never forget the swell of emotion that overcame me when I turned onto the side street that led into the square that Spaso House dominated. As soon as the buildings parted at the edge of the open space, it was impossible to focus on anything other than the Stars and Stripes rippling in the glare of three spotlights on the lawn of the mansion. For this evening, at least, I wouldn't be half a planet from home.

I produced my passport for the Marine who was standing in the guard house at the side of the wrought-iron gates. I was feeling quite giddy by the time he snapped a salute and held the gate open for me. Posh cars with diplomatic license plates were pulling up to deliver other guests—men in well-polished dress shoes and women in strappy pumps. (I was developing a fixation about shoes! They certainly weren't going to be pulling off dripping boots in the coatroom.)

They weren't—but others were. Several pairs of boots were drying on racks under damp coats in the wardrobe, and another woman, bless her, was standing in stockinged feet pulling dressy heels out of a canvas bag when I walked in. She eyed my bag and boots, and we both laughed out loud. Best of all, she turned out to be another journalist, a reporter for Cox News Service who was chief of bureau in Moscow. Right there, we forged a friendship that lasted the duration of my time in Russia.

Once I'd shed my outerwear (and my paranoia about them), I had a chance to take in the elegance of three-hundred-year-old Spaso House. Floor-to-ceiling windows in the reception area, where stewards were serving wine, showcased the front lawn and the flag. Glass in hand, I walked around the public rooms which were spare and modern in decor and furnishings. The walls were painted bold colors that set off striking examples of abstract art which I later learned were on loan to the State Department from American artists. I had been expecting the headache-inducing gilt and glitter of most of the tsarist palaces I'd visited in Russia. Instead I found cool, classic elegance.

"Do you like it?" I turned to face a small, blonde woman who immediately introduced herself as Alice Pickering and shook hands as firmly as she fixed her gaze on me. "You must be the new PIR from California."

"This house is the longest continually occupied ambassador's residence in Moscow," she said as she led the way to the candle-lit mahogany-paneled library where round tables for six were set with elegant red, white, and blue china, flowers and tablecloths reaching the floor. The room was as warm and intimate as the rest of the rooms had been cool and spare. Off to the side I caught a glimpse of a curving red-carpeted staircase leading up to a second-floor mezzanine. Could that have been the one that inspired a memorable scene in Bulgakov's *The Master and Margerita?*

As we talked, the ambassador led the rest of the guests into the room and began pointing out place cards. He noted that we would be tablemates. He pulled out a chair for me at the table nearest the tall, double-casement windows overlooking a lighted garden and began introducing me to the guests who joined us. I learned that I had the Canadian ambassador (who had no dinner partner) at my right and, at my left, the wife of a Russian diplomat who smiled broadly when I told her I was from San Francisco. She said her husband opened the consulate on Green Street in San Francisco in the seventies, the only diplomatic post they had never wanted to leave.

As soon as we were seated, the ambassador rose and offered a toast in Russian and then encouraged us to enjoy the California wine, which he teased was being served in my honor.

During the evening, I heard him speak French to the woman at his left and Russian to the diplomat at his right. I was impressed. Relations between the U.S. and Russia at that time were prickly at best; surely this man and his very able wife would navigate these rough waters as well as anyone could hope.

I wish I could say that the dinner table conversation sparked with intellectual grit, but instead I learned that the ambassadors' wives (the ambassadors at the party were all men) spent most of their time lunching and shopping and knew almost nothing about living in Moscow. They could as well have been in Istanbul or Lima—except it was colder. No one at my table could identify with the life I was living in Moscow and had no interest in sampling it.

They were mildly curious that the ambassador introduced me as a published author but talk about the book and the aftermath of the Chernobyl catastrophe quickly petered out. A couple of times I tried to stretch my ears to pick up the chatter on the other side of the table, but the bits and pieces I got didn't sound much more riveting than on my side.

By the time the guests were moving toward the door, I wasn't the least bit bothered about having to change into my boots for the trip home. If I had brought the tights, I'd have pulled them on too. Several guests waiting for their cars and drivers offered to "drop me," but by now I was perversely proud of the twenty-minute walk ahead of me.

As I started across the square, I glanced back at the flag one last time and then headed for Stariy Arbat. It was late and only a few people were about, but the street was bright, the wind had died down and huge snowflakes had begun to float down. I turned up my face to feel them settle on my cheeks and in my eyelashes with only occasional glances down to secure my footing. I'd had a marvelous night, and I was glad to be going home.

AS SOON AS I had negotiated the locks of my flat and set my boots to dry under the radiator, I pressed the space bar to wake up my Mac Powerbook 140 on the little desk in the bedroom. Checking e-mail had become a comforting part of my coming home ritual. This time I had notes from Laurie, both Robyn and David, and Anna Sharogradskaya in St. Petersburg.

I could feel the disappointment in Laurie's description of the stalled warehouse automation project in Stockton.

"There's no way I can make a trip to see you until May at the earliest. Maybe I can go back with you when you come home at Easter"—which, I noted, was exactly forty-four days away. I wanted to tell myself that that project was absorbing more of his energy because I was ten thousand miles away but that was a lie. Ever since he'd been laid off, it seemed that his very worth as a human being was tied up in getting another job where he could demonstrate his value.

Unfortunately, he may have taken on an impossible task with this project. He truly was inventing the wheel here and each step forward was followed by two steps back. It was even costing him a visit with his sister.

"Jeannie wanted to surprise me and stay here for a couple weeks while you're gone. She bought her airline ticket from Kansas City before she called me, but I had to tell her that I would be in Stockton for nearly her whole stay. I can't get away."

I replied to his message with all the right words to shore up his sagging self-worth, but I knew that those words would have had far more impact if they were spoken pillow-to-pillow rather than flickering screen-to-flickering screen. The guilt that I had done something so dramatic, so wrenching, just for me, welled up again, and I swore to make it all up to Laurie in the coming years.

I gave him a detailed account of the dinner at Spaso House and threw in a report on my latest conquest.

"I finally found the replacement filters for my Brita in a shoe store in GUM (the government department store on Red Square during Soviet times and now a sort of mall)! Now if I could only find some navy blue shoe polish. You have to polish your shoes here to preserve them, and my navy heels really need help. But I can't find any navy shoe polish in any of my usual shops. I probably have been looking in the wrong stores. If water filters are sold in a shoe store, maybe I should start looking for polish in the meat market. Lots of yellow shoe polish, but no navy."

I knew the water filter story would draw a smile from Laurie. He'd been with me when we visited our friend Oleg's apartment in Tscherbinka, an *elektrichka* ride from downtown Moscow. In the kitchen window stood a huge jar full of water, clear on top and very murky at the bottom. Oleg picked up on Laurie's curiosity about the water jug.

"We fill that with water from the faucet. After the heavy metals have settled, we ladle out the clear water on the top and boil it. Then we put it in the refrigerator, and it's ready to drink."

A year later Oleg stayed at our San Mateo home on his first visit to the U.S. He asked for a glass of water. I took out a glass and filled it with water from the tap and handed it to him. He held the glass for some time before he looked up at us.

"That's what Americans mean when they ask if you can drink the water in Russia? I always thought that was a pretty odd question. Of course, you can drink the water. You have to drink the water! But now I get it: Can you drink the water right out of the faucet?"

Not likely.

The advent of Brita water filters had simplified life for ex-pats like me, but only if we could find replacement filters. My search for them (and navy blue shoe polish) provided ample opportunity for me to honor the commitment I'd made to myself when I arrived in Moscow: Every day I would do one thing I had never done before. It might be as simple as asking for something new at a shop, dickering over the price of *shampanskoye* at a kiosk, or asking directions from a stranger. Small things, but I would be forced to stretch myself, to test what I was capable of on this Great Adventure.

WHEN I WASN'T feeling quite so brave, I could always depend on the hard currency grocery store on the street level of the next apartment building south on the *naberezhnaya* (embankment). You had to know it was there (the Press Center librarian told me about it) because, in typical Russian fashion, there was no signage. You just walked into the entry way for the building and turned left into an unmarked door. But inside was a shopper's paradise, and all you needed to come in was western currency (preferably dollars) or a credit card—which most of my neighbors certainly didn't have.

It was about the size of Ted's Grocery and Market, my folks' neighborhood store in Escondido in Southern California where I grew up, but without the great fresh meat and salad selections. The shelves were filled with the goodies you'd find in any small European shop—Swiss chocolate, German cookies, packaged cheese, tubes of Italian tomato paste, mayo and mustard (that curiously didn't have to be refrigerated after opening. I, of course, ignored that and kept them in the door of my tiny refrigerator.) A freezer was stocked with frozen chicken, steaks, and sausages of every kind.

It smelled like a grocery store: a smell I knew well from Ted's and Jewel Foods (in the Chicago suburb where I worked after we moved when I was in high school). I think it came from the oiled sawdust that my dad tossed on the floor before sweeping to keep the dust down. Mix in the odors from the ink of the price stamper and the metallic Freon of the refrigeration, and it took me back to my childhood.

One of my store jobs was to polish the fruit with a piece of chamois to make it more appealing. Anything that was less than perfect would go to our family kitchen in the back of the store. That's how I learned that a bruise or a scratch can be cut away to reveal perfectly good food. Same thing with meat. My dad was scrupulous in his presentation of chops and steaks and ground beef in the meat counter, but I could tell at a glance what we would be having for dinner—the pork roast that was going slightly brown or beef ribs with a little crust at the edges. Still perfectly delicious (and my dad would say, properly aged) but customers would ask for the pinkest, shiniest cuts. Today, I still snatch up the Manager's Specials in the meat department at Safeway—terrific selections at half the price!

My folks would leave me in charge of the store when they had to run errands from the time I was eleven or twelve. I could weigh and package meat, produce, and penny candy, run the cash register, and count change, but California law didn't allow a minor to sell cigarettes (or liquor, but we didn't stock it). So when regulars came in for cigarettes and I was alone in the store, they knew to walk around the counter, pick up their Luckies or Camels and put the correct coins on the counter. Once in a while, someone would have a bill, so I would open the till, and they'd make their own change.

My mom and dad would often drive to San Diego to stock up at the wholesale store to save the cost of the thirty-five-mile delivery. One December when I had just turned thirteen, they packed up my brother and took off in a rare Southern California rain storm for the hour's drive south. About two hours later, my dad called from a pay phone to say that the bridge on Highway 395 across the dry lake bed of "Lake" Hodges was flooded, and they couldn't get home. No worries (there hadn't been a single customer all morning because of the downpour)—except for the fact that Dad's weekly meat delivery was due soon. My dad said the delivery driver would haul the hindquarter of beef to the cutting block behind the meat counter, but I would have to cover it with the wet cloths to keep it from drying out until he got home.

Three hours later, they still weren't home, and that hindquarter, worth several hundred dollars (and weighing about seventy pounds), was wrapped in wet towels on the cutting block and needing to be in the meat cooler right away. I knew my dad was worrying himself sick about it, and I couldn't help much. It wasn't just the weight at issue: The meat cooler was below the display counter, and the opening was no more than eighteen inches high and thirty inches wide. I considered lining the floor with towels and pushing the huge slab onto the floor and then shoving it into the cooler. But I could see it was too big to get through the cooler door.

Then my dad called again, and his voice was thready. Even at thirteen, I knew we were living pretty close to the edge, and I suspected this was a loss that could push us over. He asked me if I thought I could cut it in half. I was pretty sure I could use one of his super-sharp butcher knives to cut through the meat, but cutting through the bone would require the power saw that hung from the ceiling on pulleys, the very saw that my brother and I had to stand far away from when dad used it, the very one we'd been warned a hundred times to steer clear of, the one whose noise was enough to send me running to the back of the house.

But my dad's quavering voice and my mom's silence told me that I needed to try. With the telephone receiver resting on the counter and my dad shouting instructions, I tied one of his clean aprons around myself (two times around) and unwrapped the hindquarter. Dad told me to look for the fold under the big joint and push it so the leg was sticking out at a right angle. Then I had to get the step ladder I used for "facing" the shelves of canned goods and climb up to reach the saw. Once I pulled it down, my dad told me how to stand (now on two full cartons of Clorox bleach that hadn't been unpacked yet), squeeze the switch on the saw, and pull it down through the bone.

With dad's goggles covering my glasses (and slipping down my nose) and sheer terror seizing the muscles in my back, I pulled the whining saw down through the bone with such force that I cut a wedge in the chopping block that was known for as long as we owned the store as "Micki's cut." The saw had a deadman's switch so it stopped spinning as soon as I released my finger and jerked back up to the ceiling, spraying blood all over the meat counter.

But I'd done it! I told Mom I'd made a real mess and, for perhaps the only time in my life, she told me not to worry about it. Now I had two pieces of beef that I could push off the cutting block onto clean towels and shove into the cooler. By the time my folks got home after midnight, I'd even cleaned up most of the blood spray.

ANNA HAD AN invitation for me. The seminars in St. Petersburg had gone so well she suggested another series in other cities in the Leningrad region, starting with Novgorod, the first capital of Russia and home of the oldest Russian Orthodox Church.

Of course!

Two weeks later, the temperature was hovering near freezing at 5 a.m. when I met Anna and our driver outside the Hotel Moskva for the three-hour car trip to Novgorod. Because train and bus schedules didn't mesh well with the seminar time frame, Anna had hired a private car and driver for the trip. The driver proved to be very "private"—the ever popular "friend of a friend" who needed the extra cash and who had repaired the heater in the tiny red-orange Lada especially for this trip.

It was pitch black with no sign of morning when we crawled into the back seat, poked scarves into the hole where the door handle had been, wrapped up in blankets, and prepared to sleep for a good portion of the journey. There wasn't much traffic—especially headed out of St. Petersburg—and I was soon lurched and lulled into a welcome dream.

I remember the car slowing and then stopping but neither Anna nor I bothered to raise up and look around—at least not until the driver opened the back door and lifted the blanket.

"If you please, you should get out of the car. It's burning."

Oh, I was very awake now! Anna and I scrambled out of the car next to our bags which the driver had been so kind as to unload before he woke us. The car was burning all right—not just smoke but major flames were licking out from under the hood which was half raised. The driver was filling a basin with snow and then dumping the snow on the flames. Anna joined in while I picked up our bags and moved a fair distance away from the car. Throwing snow on a blazing engine didn't seem too promising to me, but in fact the flames died down to a smolder and finally, with one last basinful of snow, went out.

Anna and I wrapped ourselves in the blankets and stamped our feet in the snow while the driver fanned the smoke. After a while he tried the starter and the engine actually turned over. The car lurched forward a few feet and died again.

The driver said he was going to try to limp back to St. Petersburg. Would we come with him? "Of course not!" Anna answered. We were due in Novgorod at 9 a.m., and we would hitch a ride to the nearest town and take a bus.

He shrugged and got back in the car. Several more lurches and he was turned around and crawling back the way we had come. Unfortunately for hitchhikers, all the traffic was going into St. Petersburg; the cars going our way were passing at very broad intervals—and all passing. Two women in dark coats alongside the highway in predawn darkness weren't attracting the appropriate attention—and it was very, very cold.

My blessing, if there was a blessing to be found, was that I didn't have to find a way out. I had Anna—who was as "in charge" by the side of this frozen highway as she was in her office in St. Petersburg—and she wasn't going to let me freeze to death on her watch!

As the horizon began to lighten a bit, we realized that we weren't actually in the middle of nowhere. Just off the highway was a small village of perhaps eight or ten cottages. I couldn't tell what color they were, but experience told me they were either bright green or bright blue with heavy white "gingerbread" shutters. The cottages or *izba* in European Russia always looked as if they had just leaped off the pages of a book of fairy tales. And almost invariably they were green or blue, perhaps the full range of colors available at the local paint store. When I first started traveling in Russia, I found the cottages particularly charming and wondered why anyone would willingly abandon one for the *khruschovki*—the sterile, concrete apartment blocks that began to dot the outskirts of every Soviet city during the Khrushchev era. A Russian friend explained that what the flats lacked in "charm" they made up for in conveniences—such as running water and indoor bathrooms which the *izba* sadly lacked.

As we tried to evaluate which cottage offered the best hope of salvation, a light flickered on in one about fifty yards from the highway and soon a thin trail of smoke wisped from the chimney. Anna steamed ahead as I grabbed the bags and tried to follow in her footsteps across the fresh snow.

By the time I got to the cottage, Anna was already chatting up a sleepy-eyed young woman through the door which was opened only a crack. I hung back, unsure of whether I was to be the "ace in the hole" or the unwelcome surprise. Oh, yes, by the way, you don't mind that I have an American woman with me who perhaps could come in and warm herself next to your stove, do you?

Whatever she said, it worked. The woman opened the door, and we kicked the snow from our boots and stepped into the mud porch outside the kitchen. We pulled off our boots and hustled into the welcome warmth of the house. A tea kettle was steaming on the wood stove, and a child about two or three was standing in the doorway to the front room. A small room off the kitchen to the left apparently was the bedroom, the only other room in the cottage. We'd passed the outhouse in the yard on our way from the highway.

Turns out I was the ace in the hole. Anna convinced this young woman that the rules of international hospitality required that she let this middle-aged *Amerikanka* rest by her fire while Anna found us a ride to Novgorod. While I sipped tea and chatted with this doe-eyed woman and her baby, Anna left to find the only telephone in the village. The shell-shocked look never left the young woman's face as she heated *kasha* (porridge) and sliced bread. Her son, Alyosha (a diminutive of Alexey), soon overcame his shyness and climbed onto my lap to look at his picture books. He seemed particularly attentive when I was speaking and I was sure he understood every word I said until he turned to his mother and asked, "What does she say?" Oh, well.

By the time Anna returned, the young woman and I were well-acquainted. I'd shown her photos of my children and explained the best I could what I was doing before dawn in the middle of a Leningrad wood in the dead of winter. Her name was Katya and she was twenty-two. She told me that she and her little boy lived alone in this cottage which had belonged to her grandmother before she died. The boy had no father, she said, and I got no further details. Anna was back—with transportation!

Boots back on and warmed inside with tea and *kasha*, I hoisted the bags and slogged after Anna across the snow to the highway where a World War II vintage truck with a camouflage paint job was waiting. The truck was carrying railroad workers to a construction site about an hour down the road toward Novgorod, and we were welcome to take a seat on one of the wooden benches stretched across the bed of the truck under a drafty canvas cover. The only light forced its way through mud-speckled isinglass windows.

The workmen were as surprised to be sharing their space with us as Katya was to have me in for tea. But their shock was lubricated by a communal supply of vodka that was passed around for us to share. I was so cold I was tempted to take a swig but Anna pushed it away, and we bounced on—unlubricated and bitterly chilled—for nearly an hour.

Limbs stiff with cold, we climbed off when the truck jerked to a stop by the side of the road. A short distance down another road was a bus station which, we were assured, would soon have a bus heading for Novgorod. Anna strode off, and I struggled on behind her. The bus station surely did have bus service to Novgorod but it wouldn't get us there until noon. It was already after nine but noon was unacceptable.

Anna left me and the bags at the bus station. She was gone so long I was just about convinced that she actually had decided to chuck it all and go back to St. Petersburg—without me. But when she did show up, she had a car—a real car, a Jeep Cherokee which I had never before seen in Russia and wouldn't soon see again. No matter that the car had no back seat. Anna and I shared a bucket seat in front while the young driver took off for Novgorod with the authority that only a fine-running western car can provide in Russia. I knew Anna had paid a king's ransom for this limo ride, but we would be in Novgorod before noon—a full hour before noon.

When we finally straggled into the conference room, every seat was occupied by an eagerly expectant editor waiting silently for pearls of design wisdom to fall from my lips.

I asked for tea, very hot tea, spread out my materials and started in. *"Menya zavoot Michelle Carter. . . ."* I don't remember anything else about the ancient city of Novgorod; all I remember is that we got there—somehow—without frostbite.

At each stop along the dog-and-pony circuit, I had begun to find an occasional gem, an example of great newspaper design that was perfectly suited to the Russian medium. I started collecting them so I could show Russian editors what other Russian designers were doing that really worked. They were much more likely to buy what I was selling if they could see effective design in a Russian context. I called it "cross-pollinating."

Once I had about twenty examples in hand, I e-mailed the editor of the Society of Newspaper Design magazine and pitched a story focused on Russian newspapers. The story was spread over five pages in the Spring edition with fifteen pages from my stash:

"Want to get in on the ground floor in newspaper design? Come to Russia! Here's a country where newspapers are flexing muscles that haven't been used in seventy-five years, testing the ever-changing limits of new freedoms of expression . . .

"Good newspaper design is beginning to happen in Russia. As with everything else in this huge country, the process is uneven.

Some of the most creative-looking papers have died while some design dinosaurs lumber on. There's a second revolution going on here with plenty of chaos. As usual, the newspapers reflect it all."

The idea was so appealing to the brass at SND that they invited me to come to the international convention in Barcelona, Spain, the first week in September, to talk about newspaper design in Russia. I e-mailed YES! in all-caps, and then dashed off a note to Laurie telling him to start polishing his Spanish. We were going to Barcelona!

Letters From Russia
It's the babushki who really run Russia

MOSCOW — A stock character in any good Russian story is the *babushka* (with the accent on the first syllable, not the second). She's the grandmother (or simply the old woman) who has lived long enough to tell the rest of the world what to do—loudly and often.

The same *baba* cooing to her grandchild on the park bench can be transformed in an instant into a harpy tugging at the miniskirt of a totally unknown young girl and screaming at her to stop dressing like a whore. The pious old crone in the Russian Orthodox cathedral who mumbles unheard prayers and smiles beneficently at the priest can be remarkably spry about pulling the ear of a young congregant who happens to slip his hands into his pockets.

I've had any number of run-ins with the "*baba*" generals who give no ground to foreigners who don't know enough to stand in the right queue to pay for bread or don't have a loop inside the coat collar so it can be hung properly on the hook in the coatroom, who walk through the wrong side of the turnstile or try to stick a telephone token in the Metro slot.

But I've learned to respond to the tirade of abuse with one of those Russian trademarks—the shrug. No argument, no smart comeback. Just a shrug, *baba;* you do your thing and I'll do mine.

I've developed the shrug into an art form, but I still will walk across streets (through Moscow traffic!) to avoid a *babushka* who's clearly in an ill mood. So you can imagine my discomfort last Sunday when I found myself surrounded by an entire coven of them on a train platform in a downpour.

I was waiting for the *electrichka* to take me to visit friends in Tscherbinka, south of Moscow. It was the first time I'd made the trip on a weekend, and I was unprepared for the swarms of people who were crowded under the tin roof of the station. I also was confused by the schedule, which seemed to indicate there would be two trains arriving at the station at the same time, but only one would stop at Tscherbinka.

Since signage hasn't yet caught on in Russia, I knew I couldn't depend on the train displaying its destination. You just had to know—and I didn't.

As I pondered the situation, I realized I was in the middle of a sea of clucking, tsk-ing old women, most of them with henna-ed red hair. I felt like a giant since not one of them was taller than my shoulder, and I hadn't escaped their notice. They were chattering about me.

Finally, one (a platinum blonde with serious roots) looked up at me and said sternly, "*Otkuda?*" "Where are you from?" I replied that I was an American from California and there was an immediate hum and unison nodding of heads. I added that I lived in Moscow now.

Now the hum turned to an excited buzz. They all had questions, but the blonde was still the spokesperson. She wanted to know why I lived in Moscow, where was I going now and why would I want to go Tscherbinka? I answered patiently, and then I added that I had a problem. I didn't know which train would stop there.

"I will show you!" said the blonde who introduced herself as Olga.

Just about then a train pulled in, and Olga started shoving me forward. It seemed as if thousands had the same idea, but I had become a "project" for the women. They were going to get this *Amerikanka* on this train, no matter what.

Olga pushed and two others pulled, and I squeezed into the car, which was jammed with families on Sunday outings. Once inside I discovered that Olga had ordered a couple of teenagers out of their seats and had reserved a spot for me.

She chattered and I listened for about twenty minutes, and then she told me Tscherbinka was the next stop. I tried to get up and start moving toward the door, but I wasn't making any progress. Olga motioned for me to push, but I obviously didn't have the right *babushka* moves.

So Olga took charge. She climbed up on her seat and began shouting, "Make way for the *Amerikanka*. Let her out. Show her that Russians are good people who respect foreigners."

It wasn't like the parting of the Red Sea, but people boosted me along and out onto the landing just before the doors closed. As the train lurched forward, Olga was in the window cheering my success.

All these Cold War years, we may have believed that it was those wooden men lined up in front of Lenin's Tomb in Red Square who pulled the strings. But I've no doubt now it was the *babas* who really ran the show.

Chapter Six

ON THE WALL of my tiny kitchen, the Ansel Adams calendar with the breathtaking black-and-white photos of the Sierra Nevada shouted SPRING! even if the views from my window did not. I crossed every day off with a big, black "X" the morning after. I'm rarely superstitious but somehow the idea of checking off the day before bed with still another two or three hours of "dayness" seemed to be toying with fate. So the calendar check-off became part of my waking ritual.

It was no longer pitch dark at seven when the alarm went off. I had made it to the halfway point between the winter and summer solstices in these northern latitudes. The days were now of fairly normal length and rushing headlong toward the white nights of summer. Now it was easier for me to get out of bed, into my down slippers and robe, and into the kitchen where I flipped on the radio on top of my neat little German refrigerator.

The radio was tuned to the BBC which broadcast on AM for two hours mornings and evenings, and it was the only source of English-language broadcasting that came into my flat. My television showed only Russian-language programming. Although cable (with CNN and other shows in English) was widely available in Moscow, my landlady couldn't see why she should ask the owner of the building to allow a cable connection on the roof. I already had five channels! Why would I need any more?

But I needed to hear English. I craved it! Once I changed seats on the bus to move closer to two men speaking English. I wasn't interested in what they were saying; I just wanted to hear their speech. To hear someone speaking English made me feel less isolated and a bit less homesick. I'm sure it was part of the reason for my Sunday splurge—the western breakfast buffet at the Radisson Slavyanskaya Hotel across the river from my flat. The Slavyanskaya had created an American enclave in this high-rise block next to the Kiev railway station. Drop by the Slavyanskaya and you could get American food, watch current-release Hollywood films in English (complete with popcorn!), change dollars to rubles, buy western newspapers, and listen to spoken English.

On Sunday mornings I would allow myself this retreat to my American roots. I'd walk across the Borodinsky Bridge (the one Muscovites were always warning me against lest I be assaulted by Gypsy hordes) and charge an outrageous fifteen dollars to my credit card for fresh fruit, croissants, bacon, scrambled eggs, hash browns, coffee, and the *International Herald Tribune*. My nose would be in the paper but mostly I listened since the dining room was always filled with American businesspeople. Sometimes I wanted to shout, "Don't think for a minute that this is really Russia!" But it was hard to feel smug when I was there because I hungered for English as much as for the American breakfast.

For the rest of week, it was up to the BBC to satisfy my lust for English and, in the process, it morphed me into a sort of hybrid European. Every morning I listened to the news of the day from a decidedly British slant, and I appreciated the European perspective on such topics as Bosnia and American reluctance to send troops to defend American interests abroad. How could the United States behave like the Number One world power in economics and trade and then refuse to dirty itself when things got messy? Such sentiments crept into one of my *San Mateo Times* newspaper columns and a Letter to the Editor writer asked what was happening to me "over there."

Besides the news, every morning I got a dose of culture as well. The BBC broadcast half-hour segments of radio dramatizations of classic novels by Jane Austen and the Brontes or an Agatha Christie mystery. I hadn't listened to radio drama since I was a child in a house where the soap operas of Helen Trent ("Can a mature woman find happiness in a small mining town in the West?") whined on in the background, but now I found myself setting my alarm, even on days when I didn't have to be in the office early, so I wouldn't miss an episode.

I would sit at my kitchen table (which was small enough to fit into a child's playhouse), breakfast on tea and toast, listen to the perils of Pauline or Prudence or Portia and count the days until Easter, when I'd make a ten-day visit home.

But first comes Lent. Laurie sent a detailed report of the Shrove Tuesday (or Fat Tuesday or *Mardi Gras*) celebration at church, the day before Ash Wednesday, which always included a pancake supper. In the Orthodox tradition here, the holiday is *Maslenitza* or Butter Week when all the butter, sugar, and sweets are eaten up in anticipation of Lenten fasts. Everyone was having *Maslenitza* parties with rich cakes and desserts, and one of my neighbors left a poppy seed roll wrapped in paper in front of the door of my flat. At the Press Office party, everyone brought *blini* (those sugared pancakes eaten with sweetened cottage cheese) with all kinds of exotic fillings. Plain old American pancakes were pretty dull by comparison.

THE PARTIES PROVED to be an appropriate send-off for me since I was heading to the ancient city of Nizhny Novgorod (called Gorky during the Soviet period) for four days of daylong seminars. Three came off without a hitch, but on the last day, one of the editors stormed out of the room, shouting that I was wasting his time with nonsense, that he had serious matters to attend to. I soldiered on, but his noisy exit had cast a pall.

For many Russians, I'd learned over several trips, almost anything American was shallow and insipid. My friend Oleg and I had talked about this often. Part of the problem was that few Americans had the skills to get around Russia by themselves. In France or Italy, tourists may not understand the language, but at least they can read the Metro map and the names of the stops. But in Moscow, they can rarely do that. So opportunities to meet ordinary Russians outside the cloistered hotels and guided tours are few.

As a result, most saw Americans as loud and grinning tourists who moved about the country insulated from the daily Russian experience—or the image created from the American things they had around—detective novels instead of great literature, T-shirts, jeans, pornographic films. (During the Cold War, the Soviet Union certainly had no interest in importing the best America had to offer.) So Russians believed America had no substance because what they had seen of America had no substance.

But there was more to the image problem than cheap American goods. It had a lot to do with the Russian "soul" which craves deep philosophical and political dialogue. Last month, I'd had this same discussion at a Moscow dinner party in a crowded apartment. Cheek by jowl, we squeezed onto sofas or pulled cushions to the floor with plates of food on our laps. We hashed over Yeltsin's lack of political muscle (and public drunkenness), Clinton's role in Bosnia, and even the European song festival as most slugged back vodka, smoked cigarette after cigarette, and argued until dawn. My eyes were smarting and I was craving sleep (and, Lord knows, I can't drink vodka), but the debate got heated, even vitriolic, and I had to hold my own.

One of Oleg's favorite childhood memories, he told me, was going with his grandfather to the public baths where he would listen to truck drivers and bricklayers grapple with politics and poetry as a pastime. "Americans don't share this passion for wrestling with philosophical issues. It contributes to their shallow image among Russians."

I knew he was right. I had discovered, quite by surprise, that I could pierce the crusty shell of Soviet-era editors with a few lines of Russian poetry I had memorized when I was a student of Russian, learning proper pronunciation. At a one-day seminar in the ancient Golden Ring city of Suzdal, a young page designer brought me over to his hard-edged editor (the image of a burly, barrel-chested Leonid Brezhnev), who clearly didn't want to be there at all, in the hope that I could convince him to allow the designer a little freedom.

Think of design as the art and romance of newspapering, I told him. Give the young designer some room to find his creative spirit, like Lermontov. *Vyhozhu odin ya na dorogu . . .* I launched into a familiar piece by the much beloved Romantic poet.

He beamed at me, and we finished the poem together. The ice was broken, and I could do no wrong from that moment on. That poem had wedged open a crack I was able to slip through. It might even have worked on the editor in Nizhny if I'd have gotten the chance.

TECHNICALLY, I WOULD be in the States for one of two USIA debriefings my contract called for. (The other was scheduled for my Labor Day holidays.) In fact, I was ticketed to San Francisco with a ten-day layover, then to Washington, D.C. for two days where

I would meet with my new USIA handler, Valerie Kreutzer, and then back to Moscow. But all my energy was focused on getting home after fourteen very long, dark weeks. Laurie's most recent e-mails were still full of depressing reports on the warehouse automation project. The scanners were sending garbled information, and the vendors hadn't been able to come up with a workable fix. Meanwhile, the Del Monte brass was pushing to go live as soon as possible.

He'd told them that he would be taking some time off to spend with me in Moscow but he didn't feel he could leave until the glitches were solved. He wouldn't be coming back with me in April. I'd been expecting this but it still sucker punched me.

His supervisor also mentioned that they might ease up on the hiring freeze in the summer and put him on salary with benefits.

"I know you think they're just toying with me, but they're paying out as much to the temp agency for me as they'd pay if I was on salary with benefits. Maybe more. And if they think they're getting more out of me because I don't have job security, they don't know me as well as they ought to."

No, after twenty-eight years, Del Monte still didn't know that this was a unique man who would give everything he had all the time, every time, because he was as good as his word. I don't know how many times, over the years, people had told me that with Laurie, what you see is what you get! He had no pretense, no artifice. I know some of my newspaper acquaintances, as jaded and cynical as journalists come, thought my husband was uncomplicated and unsophisticated, perhaps even simple. To me and to our friends, he was direct and as good as his word.

We attended the Congregational Church of Belmont for fourteen years before he was certain he could, in all honesty, repeat the affirmation of faith required of new members. The pastor suggested a number of times that Laurie could make his statement of faith in private any time he wanted, but that was the problem—the statement of faith. He had to be absolutely certain that he believed every word he was saying before he could repeat that phrase. He was "all in" with a one hundred percent commitment to anything he undertook.

During those fourteen years he worked as hard as any member ever did, singing in the choir, playing the organ, cleaning up after church events, even serving as a greeter (when meeting new people required him to overcome his deeply rooted shyness). When he finally did join, it was quite an event—in our family and in the life of the church.

MY EASTER TRIP home was still a month away when I poked my hand into the cubby hole high above my head that was my office mail box and grasped something . . . wet! I pulled out a small super-fragrant nosegay of tiny white flowers, so fresh they were still damp. I had always been a patsy for fresh flowers but, in the last few weeks, I had been aching for my California garden where I knew azaleas, camellias, and calla lilies were in full bloom. Then out of the frozen slush of a Moscow morning came these mysterious white flowers.

"Ah, so you've found our little *podsnezhniki*," Svet said as he walked into the room. "They grow in the forest near my *dacha*. When they poke up through the snow, they are the first announcement of spring although, of course, it doesn't look like spring will ever come this morning. In fact, that's where they get their name: *pod*—under, and *sneg*—snow. They come from under the snow and offer us hope."

Later, I saw *babushki* all over the city selling these little bouquets (which I later learned were called Snow Drops in America) in honor of International Women's Day on March 8. They smelled like jasmine, and I held them under my nose all the way upstairs to my office. Until that morning, I'd never heard of International Women's Day, and I found it more than a little ironic that this culture would put so much store by a single, official holiday for women, on one hand, and treat women so shabbily every other day of the year.

Russian society was built on the backs of women who labored, day in and day out. As little girls, they were carefully taught to serve their brothers and fathers while learning to flirt and tease to attract a spoiled man/boy whom they would marry while still in their teens. Then, as their husbands indulged themselves in vodka, cigarets, and night-long kitchen table bouts of deep, philosophical ramblings, they would rear their own daughters to serve and flirt or their sons to expect servitude and flirtation as little princes of Russia.

My daughter Robyn, who would spend time with me in Moscow in September, saw it as a "binary madonna/whore categorization system" that labeled all women as saints (most often their mothers) or sinners and treated them that way. She'd seen it in immigrant communities in the U.S., but it seemed to be the norm in Russia.

Women would work full time, commute an hour or more by bus and Metro morning and evening, shop on the way home, prepare meals, clean, supervise homework, and fall into an exhausted stupor only to get up the next morning and do it again. Women in Russia were old by forty and ancient by fifty. Of course, men in Russia were dead by sixty and, finally, the women would get some peace.

You know I'm generalizing here. I could give you fifteen exceptions to this picture, right off the top of my head. But I've seen the pattern over and over in all the years I've been traveling in Russia. On the Metro, I study the bone-weary faces of women who, I now know, are ten years younger than I am! They rub swollen, misshapen feet if they can find a seat. I've seen those feet in mid-journey on women in their twenties and thirties who clatter around on the cobblestone and concrete of Moscow in three-inch heels carrying overstuffed shopping bags—until one day when they are too worn out and too old to care.

I once asked a co-worker why she didn't wear more comfortable shoes for walking. She sighed and smiled indulgently. "When I stop wearing these, I will be old. As long as I can walk in them, I will be young."

Perhaps the Great Patriotic War (as World War II is known in Russia) spawned this lifelong need to be sexy and flirtatious. The Soviet Union lost more than twenty-six million people, most of them men of marrying age—an entire generation of men—so maybe it's understandable that women felt the need to compete for the few men left. Maybe it was a way to subvert the mechanical, emotionless, overly structured society of the Soviet period. Maybe it was a way to exercise power!

But as dear as many of these women are to me, I've never learned to understand their willingness to play this role. To me, Russia's women are the strongest women on earth. Each one is the Motherland Calls, the Statue of Liberty-sized monument of Mother Russia clutching a scythe and flag that dominates the war memorial in Volgograd. These women are fierce in the protection of their families and their country (the Motherland, of course). They carry the country, quite literally, on their backs while they prop up weak-willed leaders who make their decisions and direct their lives.

I knew so many strong women in Russia and the former Soviet Union, Anna Sharogradskaya in St. Petersburg, Imbi Reet Kaasik in Tallinn, Tanya Patina who became my Moscow "family" while I lived there and, of course, Olga Aleinikova, the pediatric oncologist in Minsk who was the heroine of my first book on the Children of Chernobyl, the generation of children sacrificed by the Kremlin to keep a dirty secret of the catastrophic 1986 explosion and fire at the Chernobyl nuclear power plant in northeastern Ukraine.

Olga was in her early forties when we met in November 1990. I was taking part in a peace exchange between the Northern California Conference of the United Church of Christ and the Soviet Peace Committee in Moscow. However, when our group of twelve arrived in Moscow, we found the city in turmoil. The wheels were coming off the Soviet Union. The Peace Committee, which had responsibility for our itinerary, wanted to get us out of Moscow as quickly as possible. Sleepy, stolid Minsk, in the Soviet republic of Byelorussia, was where they would send us and off we went, much to our dismay.

But for me, that side trip to Minsk would be one of those doors that I would walk through in my life and be forever changed. I met Olga and we were almost instantly sisters. Shortly after our group was ushered into her closet-sized office in the Byelorussian Center for Pediatric Hematology, we introduced ourselves. She heard me say that I was a journalist. Seconds later, she had a fierce grip on my arm (leaving bruises as fingerprints) that conveyed a determination that would not be denied.

"You must tell our story! You must let the world know that thousands of children are very, very sick and we need help. We need western chemotherapy drugs. We need methotrexate. We need people to know this story."

Weeks later when I was back in California, deep into family and career and tempted to put those children out of my mind, the memory of her grip on my arm triggered a response in my heart. Olga had me and, in the end, we were a formidable team. We shared the Children of Chernobyl Project of Northern California that delivered half a million dollars' worth of *medicamenty* (drugs and medical supplies) and equipment for the molecular biology lab of the spectacular new Byelorussian Center for Pediatric Oncology and Hematology in Minsk. Olga led me into that sparkling new hospital with a scarf tied over my eyes to preserve the surprise.

I interviewed some other heroines of International Women's Day soon after I arrived in January. They were lined up across the square facing the exit from the busy Arbatskaya Metro station. The crowds rushing to work couldn't miss them, their shouts, or the signs they carried. The words varied from woman to woman, but the messages were the same:

Where is my son?

These are the Mothers of the Soldiers of Russia, and they have been standing vigil in the streets of Moscow daily since the invasion of the southern autonomous region of Chechnya began, sometimes silently with the portraits of their sons held in front of them, sometimes chanting as they try to make the generals meeting inside buildings nearby aware of their presence.

The group had grown spontaneously as mothers, grandmothers, sisters, and aunts encountered each other as they tried to get information about the Russian Army units that had been sent into Chechnya in an all-out assault against other Russian sons, these with mothers in the fractious Islamic region in the south.

The first place they turned to was the tiny and frigid basement office of the Mothers of the Soldiers of Russia, who organized themselves in 1989 to secure some rights for the young draftees who were often the victims of *dedovschina* (institutionalized hazing). A month earlier the committee had shape-shifted into the opposition to the Chechen war and the walls of the office had been plastered with bits of paper.

"Andrey Potronov of Company 2232 was taken prisoner near the village of Betshik. Not wounded."

"Has anyone heard news of Sasha Davidov (photo attached)?"

Families turned to the Mothers group because they couldn't get any information about their sons from the Russian Ministry of Defense. The traditional telegram announcing the death of a soldier in battle had been lost—among a dozen other civilities—in this nasty war.

Other mothers had climbed on buses or trains and made their way to Chechnya to try to find their sons and bring them home. Some had succeeded, and their stories encouraged others to do the same. When they returned, they brought the names of the soldiers they had met or heard about to the basement office. The mothers were demanding to be noticed. They were a visible representation of the discomfort most Muscovites felt about this war of Russians against Russians. But the mothers would be satisfied with just the answer to their question: Where is my son?

International Women's Day is for Olga and Anna and Tatiana and the Mothers of the Soldiers of Russia, but they deserved so much more than just one day. But Russia isn't ready yet.

It's equally hard for Russians to understand women who live by another code. Every time I got my haircut in Moscow, the *master* (stylist) would try to convince me to cover up the white that was rapidly overtaking the blond in my hair. "You would look so young!" (Ouch!)

Their pleas to henna my hair to an auburn red raised my consciousness about women with graying hair. Once I started looking, days would go by without seeing such a woman. Even the crones who swept the churchyards with twig brooms had coal black or henna-ed hair (often with a serious case of roots). That revelation caused me to add gray hair to the list of traits that tend to mark Americans in Russia—along with good teeth, big grins, and booming voices.

BY 4:45 P.M. on one almost spring day, I was doing my reverse Mr. Rogers routine, getting back into my snow boots, my long brass-buttoned navy blue coat, scarf, hat, and gloves for the walk to the Metro at the end of Stariy Arbat when I woke to the reality that it was still daylight. Not just the slanted wisps of waning light, but real daylight.

The calendar still said March but the days were getting decidedly longer, and at a quicker pace, now that the vernal equinox was in sight. I had never paid much attention to the way the seasons affected my moods, probably since weather in California didn't change much from spring to fall and back. But in Moscow, I found myself cheered by the idea that I could walk home in daylight and soon wake up in daylight too.

But, in truth, it wasn't just the longer day that had lifted my mood. I was going to make a special stop on the way home, a treat that I only permitted myself once or twice a month. I was stopping at McDonald's on the Garden Ring (I could see those golden arches from my kitchen window!) for a Big Mac, French fries, and a chocolate malt.

I pressed into the crowd inside the overheated building and wedged into a spot with a hundred other Muscovites, dripping melting snow from my coat and boots along with everyone else. Russians aren't good at queues so it was mostly a scrum of bobbing heads, jockeying for position. Lots of commuters stopped here for a quick visit to the clean restrooms, which were still in short supply in Moscow, but most were clearly here with dinner in mind.

Finally, I inched my way up to the counter to order: The *Beek Mach* and French potatoes were pretty straightforward, but I'd never understood why the chocolate malt was a *shokolodniy koktyel*. But it was, and I felt positively triumphant carrying my American fast food home in my "perhaps" bag to enjoy at the little table in my tiny kitchen. The kicker, of course, was that I couldn't remember the last time I'd been in a McDonald's at home.

But I do remember my first trip to the first McDonald's in Moscow in 1990, just ten months or so after it opened its doors in Pushkin Square as one of the first American enterprises invited to do business in the Soviet Union. I was in Moscow on that Peace Exchange, and McDonald's Moscow was on the itinerary.

In a few months, Soviet Premier Mikhail Gorbachev would resign, and the Soviet Union would officially dissolve at a December ceremony in Minsk. That November protesters were filling the streets and jamming the entrances to the Metro stations. I was thrilled with the chance to see history in the making, and the shouting students I approached were stunned to be interviewed by a middle-aged American journalist with a camera!

However, the Moscow Peace Committee was having none of it. They got us out of Moscow as quickly as possible but not before we were delivered, a bit unceremoniously, to Pushkin Square to queue up with hundreds of very cold but very determined Muscovites at McDonald's. Press reports said more than five thousand showed up on opening day (perhaps just for the emotional jolt of seeing smiling Russian clerks urging them to have a nice day!).

Interviewing protesters in Moscow in 1990.

But Mickey D's wasn't the first American business in the Soviet Union. I remember a Baskin-Robbins Ice Cream shop in the corner of the prisonlike Hotel Moskva in Moscow on my first trip in 1988. I slipped in as often as I could on that stay and launched something of a tradition. In 1990, I was back to sample a new BR flavor called Gorba-Chocolate and, on this tour of duty in 1995, a pint of chocolate raspberry truffle Baskin Robbins Ice Cream was a treat I allowed myself to bring home most Saturdays since it was available at the hard currency shop on the Garden Ring. Baskin Robbins touted its thirty-one flavors but this shop only had two, the same two, every day I shopped—maple walnut and chocolate raspberry truffle. I went for the chocolate.

I particularly like to say the Russian word for ice cream, *morozhenoye,* out loud. You practically smacked your lips in pronouncing it, so maybe that was part of the reason I indulged my passion for it when I was in Russia. And I certainly wasn't alone. It always blew my mind to be leaning into a bitter Siberian wind, with snow whipping all around me and treacherous ice under foot, only to come upon a family seated around a white wrought-iron ice cream table and chairs on the street outside a shop, digging into bowls of *morozhenoye,* totally oblivious to the weather around them or the irony of choosing a summertime treat in the depth of winter.

PERHAPS I HAD ice cream on my mind a week earlier when I climbed the steps from Smolenskaya Metro station and emerged into the late afternoon half-light of the Garden Ring just a few blocks from my apartment. Whatever I was thinking, I wasn't paying enough attention to my surroundings. Standing on the curb, I surveyed a possible path that would get me across the street without stepping ankle-deep in the dirty slush that defined March in Moscow.

With no cars approaching, I circled to the left to avoid a very large puddle when a car that had been parked at the curb backed straight into me, sending me splat into the snowy sludge I'd been trying to avoid. I was dripping wet and filthy as I tried to get up on all fours and crawl back to the curb. Passersby pulled me to my feet and gathered up my bags as I gasped for breath and wiped the muck out of my eyes.

The driver of the car, a young *biznesman* not much older than my son David, prattled on with his apologies while the watery slush covered his very expensive Italian shoes. I wasn't really hurt (despite a nasty bruise on my right hip), but I took perverse pride in finding my Russian at the depths of my humiliation. "*Shto ty dyelaesh!*" I shouted. "What are you doing," was simple enough, but I had remembered to use the familiar tense of the verb I would have used speaking to a child—and put him in his proper place!

I refused his offer of a lift home although I would have been delighted to mess up the front seat of his pristine black Mercedes. Oh, yes, one of those clean black cars I'd been warned to avoid (because they were the ones that blow up!) had come back to bite me in the butt, but not quite the way I'd been expecting.

I spent the rest of the evening trying to clean up my long navy blue coat with the brass buttons; it was still far too cold to wear anything else. My boots, however, did not survive the accident. I scraped the mud off and rubbed on the expensive leather cleaner. I tried to dry them with my hair dryer and left them to finish the night under the radiator. In the morning they were still damp but I added a pair of athletic socks and wore them to work. It wasn't until I was sitting on the Metro on the way home that I looked down and noticed the big toe on my right foot, still in its white sock, was sticking out of my boot.

My classy California boots had made it to March—through half a Russian winter—but I went out the next morning in tennis shoes and put down a very precious one hundred and fifty dollars in western currency for a sturdy pair that would make it through the rest of my stay.

Oh, I never told Laurie or anyone at home that I'd been hit by a car in Moscow. I think the idea that a car had backed into me—while I was always so careful to watch for the ones coming toward me—was too much to bear. Unfortunately, someone from the RAPIC office was among those who pulled me out of slush so the story of my miserable Mercedes encounter attached itself to me like a leech for months.

A FEW DAYS later, I was doing laundry in my bathtub and had just set up my folding wooden clothes rack—five thousand rubles at the Kiev Railroad Station *rynok* (market)—when my smoke alarm started beeping. I'd installed it just to please Laurie, and I had absolutely no plan for what to do if it went off.

I didn't smell smoke so I opened the door to the landing a tad and caught a whiff coming from the lift. In just a few seconds, it was puffing out enough smoke to fill the fifth-floor foyer. I slammed the door and did what I would do at home if something in my home caught fire. I grabbed the red plastic phone, turned over the receiver where I'd taped the number for police and fire and dialed.

I gave my address in my most careful Russian and told them the lift was on fire.

By the time I hung up, I could hear a commotion in the hallway. My neighbors, the ones I met when I broke the lock to my flat, were all on the landing sloshing basins of water into the lift, but the fire was crawling up the back wall and gaining oomph from the fresh air pouring in once the door was open. Right behind them were the neighbors on the other side with their pails full. The fire hissed back, sizzled and went out.

Of course, my smoke detector was still beeping its heart out. I dragged the kitchen table over, climbed up, and popped the battery out to shut it up. Then I joined the neighbors on the landing with some rags to start the cleanup. That's when I told them I'd called the fire department—and launched a real firestorm.

No, no! You never ever call the firemen, they shouted at me. They will just come and look in your apartment and see what you have for them to steal. Don't call the police either. They will steal everything.

I kept repeating how sorry I was, that I didn't know I shouldn't call. The neighbors on either side of me were sharing the pain of having to explain the realities of life to the *Amerikanka* when we heard the sirens. In an instant, they scuttled like June bugs into their flats, slammed the doors and snapped all the deadbolts. I stood there, holding sopping towels and gaping, trying to take in what had just happened.

I heard the firemen, but I tried to send them away. I called down from the fifth floor to tell them the fire was out, that I didn't need them. Would they please go away? Not a chance. They clambered up the stairs armed with fire extinguishers and peered into the lift. However, the real object of interest was the *Amerikanka*—me. No Muscovite in her right mind would have called them for a fire in the lift.

I told them I only called because my smoke detector went off.

Now the guy in charge took over. "What's that?"

"Smoke detector. It tells me if there's a fire."

"Show me this smoke detector."

Now I knew I was in trouble. I could almost hear my neighbors, huddled behind their dead-bolted doors, clucking no, no, don't do it! But I did—and what a show it was.

Once I got the batteries back in, the firemen all crowded into my entryway and took turns setting the gizmo off by lighting matches under it and cheering it on. No doubt about it, it had to be the only smoke detector in Moscow.

It was nearly an hour before they were gone. I went back to finish cleaning up the lift. I felt responsible for the mess, somehow. I'd barely gotten back to my laundry when Team Two showed up. The commander or captain or whatever he was had decided that this was a find worth sharing. For the rest of the afternoon, firemen came up in shifts to flick their lighters under my smoke detector and chuck each other on the shoulder as it burst out beeping.

I was exhausted by the end of the day. I wasn't the least bit worried about the firemen coming back to steal me clean, but I felt awful about disappointing my neighbors. I didn't see them for days so I knew they were waiting behind closed doors until they heard me leave. Their tsk-tsking hung in the air.

JUST BEFORE I left for Russia at the first of the year, I'd gotten a call from someone in the office of the Episcopal bishopric in San Francisco. He said he had heard that I was going to Russia and wondered if I would be willing to help with a major international project.

It sounded intriguing, and it got even better when he said it was going to be part of the fiftieth anniversary celebration for the United Nations. Turns out the bishop's office was organizing an ecumenical worship service in June as part of the celebration, and they wanted to create a fountain using water from the seven great rivers of the world.

I thought I could see what was coming, and it was sounding a lot less exciting. I made non-committal noises and listened on. Would I be willing to collect some water from the Volga River in Russia and bring it back to San Francisco in time for the ecumenical service?

Not exactly James Bond stuff, but I said I'd give it a try. I thought, big river, big country. I'm going to be traveling nearby, and I'll be back in the Bay Area in April. Why not?

Any Russian, of course, would have known immediately why not, but Californians tend not to think of things by the calendar since seasons come and go on the Peninsula with a certain sameness. However, in Russia wars are won and lost depending on the season. Marriages, births (and some would say, even deaths) are planned around the seasons. As it says in Ecclesiastes, "for everything there is a season," and in Russia, the season for taking water from the Volga isn't winter.

But winter was all I had and, who knows, there might have been an international incident if water from the Volga wasn't included along with water from the Mississippi and the Nile—both "gimmies" for their collectors, as far as I was concerned.

My first shot at the task came in February when I had seminars scheduled in Nizhny Novgorod, Russia's third largest city which sits at the convergence of the Volga and the Ob rivers about two hundred miles northeast of Moscow. I told my hosts about my task; they laughed. Perhaps they could find an ice fisherman who would lower a bottle into his fish hole, they said. But they couldn't, so I bundled up and climbed down to the river's edge with an ice pick (actually a screwdriver) to see if I could get to the water. The best I could come up with was ice chips, little ice chips, from the Volga.

The only other chance I had before April was at Yaroslavl, eighty miles north of Moscow, which was on the schedule for March, late March. Surely by then the ice would be breaking up, and this time I had an accomplice. A friend from home, Mike Venturino, was coming along and willing to help.

In Yaroslavl, I got more snickers from my hosts but I managed to pique their provincial pride with the idea of having water collected at Yaroslavl, the ancient Golden Ring city of Russia, poured into a fountain in San Francisco with waters from all over the world. They borrowed a car and we drove over the river to a park that runs along the Volga embankment where we could approach the river fairly safely.

The ice was broken in a few places, and we could actually see water although getting to it didn't look promising. The walking was treacherous on a downslope of solid ice; only the thick treads of Mike's hiking boots allowed him to get to the edge of the river. He spotted a break in the ice a few yards on and crept ahead. While I recorded the event on camera, he tried to fill a plastic mineral water bottle.

Unfortunately, the "break" turned out to be about two inches of water on the surface of solid ice below. Mike scooped up as much as he could—about five ounces—and we called it a success. We had water from the Volga—or at least water that had been on top of the Volga.

Mike delivered the bottle into the hands of the Episcopalians in San Francisco, and I wondered if the person who got the water from the Nile had half the trouble we did.

The calendar page eventually did turn to April, and my Easter holiday was in sight. After a Metro trip across the city to the Lufthansa office in the hotel by the Olympic stadium (and a hike through a construction site inconveniently located between the Metro station and the hotel), I had my ticket in hand—round-trip, of course, because I would be coming back. I would complete the assignment and play out my Great Adventure 'till the end.

I would.

Letters From Russia
What's right about Russia

MOSCOW — They moved the clocks ahead last week, and I mean all of them.

In four hours (from two until dawn on a Sunday morning), the hands of every one of this city's two thousand-plus street clocks, as well uncounted thousands of clocks in every public building, were advanced one hour.

As the citizen of a country where there's rarely a street clock that works at all, I find that truly amazing.

In a city that's raised "chaos" to an art form, an entire legion of city workers planned the clock change like a military invasion. Huge charts were erected on the walls of the public works department, and each worker got his or her assignment. Then at the appointed hour, they raced to their posts with the appropriate instruments and went to work. That first Sunday morning stroller (who'd probably forgotten about "springing ahead") was confronted with the correct time of day.

All of which brings me to a discussion of what's right about this place. I've spent a fair amount of space relating Russia's foibles, but some things here DO work—consistently, efficiently, and usually without appreciation.

At the top of any such list has to be the Metro system. Stalin never thought small. When he decided that Moscow needed a subway system, he provided the resources to make it one of the wonders of the world. It would be one of those public jewels for which ordinary citizens endured private sordidness and deprivation.

Each station had a theme—ornate statuary, red marble, stained glass, gilded chandeliers—so that a passing glance at real beauty would be available to everyone in the socialist paradise. Add to that trains that run every two minutes all day long (less frequently all night) in a network of more than two hundred stations and nine intersecting lines—and they just keep going and going and going. A breakdown is a distinct rarity.

The designers of the Metro system had a terrific model to work from in the network of trains that crisscross the eleven time zones of Russia with clockwork precision.

Now these trains aren't anyone's idea of a luxury liner, but they are mostly clean, serviceable, and safe. In fact, in the last year or so, they've gotten better. The windows are getting washed, the curtains ironed—and on my last trip there was even toilet paper (well, paper of some sort) in the bathroom! That was a first.

Finally, the cultural climate of this country is astonishing. Every night of the week there's a spellbinding array of concerts, operas, ballets, plays, recitals, and exhibits. Performances always start at seven, so everyone comes right from work. These aren't dress-up occasions, and children are encouraged. Although prices are outrageous compared to the kopeks of the past, I've never paid more than about ten dollars—usually much less. In addition, there's an abundance of free performances of every sort.

Two nights ago I heard the Moscow Philharmonia play Verdi's *Requiem* with an eighty-member choir and four soloists. (My landlady is a violinist with the orchestra, and she frequently leaves me tickets at the door.) The performance was extraordinary, and every seat in the Tschaikovsky Conservatoire (where the composer himself had been a student) was filled. I was bowled over to find out that each program is given only once, and the Philharmonia prepares different programs five nights a week.

Russians like to complain, and visitors to this country can fall into the habit very quickly. After all, there's a lot to complain about. But some things—the Metro, the trains and the symphony—do work, and remarkably well.

Chapter Seven

THREE AND A half months after arriving in Moscow to start my Great Adventure, I was going home!

RAPIC's driver Gennady was dozing in the driver's seat of his yellow Lada when I rolled my suitcase out of the vestibule of the apartment building on Rostovskaya Naberezhnaya at 4:45 a.m. on April 15 and rapped on the window. He jumped out of the car and loaded my bags into the trunk as I climbed into the back seat.

It was a Saturday morning and traffic was light as we drove north across the city to Sheremetyevo Airport. Gennady usually talked non-stop when he was driving, but he was fairly quiet this time, which led me to believe that he might have had a late one the night before. It would not have been out of character for him to have come directly to my apartment at the end of his evening and napped in the car until I showed up. The motor was running, and the heater was on when I climbed in.

He did interrupt the silence to ask if I was going to meet my husband. Gennady and most Russians I worked with were fascinated with the idea that I was married, but my husband wasn't with me in Moscow. Maybe I wasn't really married at all. Maybe I just made him up so that men wouldn't pester me (as if that ever works!). Maybe the *Amerikanka* had secrets!

Would my husband and my children come back with me? Maybe . . . but probably not until June.

With Gennady, I would put up with a lot of nosy questions because a reliable driver with a car that worked (who really would show up at 4:45 a.m.!) was a treasure in a city the size of Moscow with no taxis, especially when a trip to Sheremetyevo was involved. Gennady, of course, had to know everything about the person I was meeting or where I was headed to, and he always stayed close by to haul bags or give advice—lots of advice—even if I only understood about half of what he was telling me.

He was right by my side on a terribly foggy night in March when he'd driven me out to meet Laurie's and my friend, Mike Venturino, who'd become something of a courier between home and Moscow. He was a United Airlines captain who could jump-seat on Lufthansa for free. Twice he'd carried some papers Laurie needed me to sign and refills for my Synthroid prescription (for my thyroid deficiency, a souvenir from too many trips to the Chernobyl region and one truly stupid helicopter ride over the leaking reactor).

The fog was nasty and, all the way to the airport, Gennady kept telling me there would be no airplanes tonight. Too much fog. I was beginning to believe he was right although I was pretty sure Mike would have found some way to let me know if the flight had been cancelled.

The cavernous airport was nearly empty (except for the pigeons who live year-round in the faux bronze light canisters in the ceiling) although a number of flights were still showing on the arrivals board. It continued to clatter as the rows of plastic slats flipped over every few minutes. It sounded as if everything was normal, but the visual was quite different.

We went to the Lufthansa counter to ask, but it was deserted. No luck at the gate posted for the flight either. I plopped down in the waiting area, wishing I could find some hot tea when Gennady wandered off—and probably not in search of tea.

About fifteen minutes later I heard his shout echoing down the hall. When I caught up with him, he waved me into a grubby office where several men in grease-smeared parkas were lounging about, smoking, and slugging back vodka.

Tell her, Gennady prodded them. Tell her where the plane is.

Too much fog. All Lufthansa flights go to Helsinki.

I never learned who they were, but Gennady led me out to the car in absolute certainty that they knew what they were talking about. They did. Mike arrived from Finland the next day with just a few hours to spend.

A WEEK LATER it was the Russian rail system that defeated me. I'd planned a trip to Tallinn to visit a dear Estonian friend, Imbi Reet-Kasik, a high school principal who had been an interpreter for my 1988 trip. Laurie and I'd taken the train to Tallinn several times before in previous trips. A snapshot of him in a too-short pair of sweats cinched-up around his waist, chopping wood in Imbi's garden sat on the piano in my Moscow flat.

My Russian visa allowed multiple entries and exits. No problem.

I e-mailed Laurie on a Saturday morning. I'm not in Tallinn although I said I would be—and you will never believe why! I couldn't buy a train ticket. Why?

Because I didn't have an Estonian visa.

Why didn't I get one?

Because Americans don't need a visa to travel to Estonia any more. Doesn't that sound familiar?

Even a document from the Estonian consulate—with an official stamp (and you know how much Russians love officials stamps)— wasn't enough to persuade a train agent in Moscow to sell me a ticket. She said, I don't take my orders from the Estonians, only from the train company.

So your train is going to run empty to Tallinn?

Better empty than full of illegals!

When I called Imbi to tell her, she said, now you know why we had to get away from Russia!

Imbi is another of those women that International Women's Day was meant to honor, but she would fume at the idea of being lumped together with Russians, men or women. The Soviet Union still had a firm grip on Estonia when I visited in 1988, but spitting in the eye of the Russians was a national sport. For the three days we stayed in Tallinn, a historic corner of the Hanseatic League of trade in the Middle Ages, I marveled at the banded blue-black-white Estonian flags that would hang from nearly every street-side window every morning. Soviet trucks with cherry-pickers would rumble down the streets at first light to pull those flags down, but the flags would be back the next day.

I delighted in the chance to document what I saw as heroic resistance for the readers of *The San Mateo Times*, and Imbi shuttled me into sweltering barns and abandoned factory lofts to interview those people who rebelled against the attempts to Sovietize Estonia and the other Baltic states that fell under Soviet control at the beginning of World War II. These "resisters" organized classes in the Estonian language to preserve their native tongue in the face of

Russian-only public schools and undermined Soviet plans to move thousands of Russians into Estonia to aid in its Russification.

That resistance was so fierce that it morphed into rampant nationalism when the USSR fell in 1991 and Estonia won its independence. Russians, who had lived their entire lives in Estonia, were denied citizenship in the new state.

Laurie, Mike Venturino, and I had front-row seats to that shaky transition to democracy in June 1992. We were fresh off a humanitarian trip to deliver food and medical supplies to Belarus, which was struggling to survive its new independence, when we decided on a whim to skip the two days in Moscow on our planned itinerary and take the train to Tallinn to see Imbi.

We bought tickets on the night train with no difficulties, climbed on and tried to catch some sleep. I was out almost immediately, but Laurie and Mike were still talking when the train stopped at the Estonian border. Russian passport control officers rapped on the door of our *vagon*, and we produced our *dokumenty*. We knew the routine.

We had no Estonian visas (which weren't required of Americans then either), but we weren't worried until one of the officers poked his AK-47 at us, ordered us off the train, and pointed us to a shed on the side of the tracks. Laurie and Mike were led into one room and I another. Nothing routine about this.

The issue was the absence of an Estonian visa, the same bugaboo that rose up to bite me three years later. We all protested that as Americans we didn't need one, and we were pretty sure a phone call would clear everything up.

While one guard stayed with Laurie and Mike and presumably was going to make that phone call, two others grilled me for nearly an hour about the purpose of my visit, why I had been to Minsk (the stamp on my passport was the clue), and whom would I see in Tallinn. I understood most of their questions but I decided that this was one of those moments when playing dumb might be effective. I shrugged at every question and replied, *Po-angliskii?* In English?

Gradually it dawned on me that these border guards, not much more than teenagers, weren't operatives in some sinister intrigue. They were bored, stuck at a distant border in the middle of the night, and had decided to interrogate a twitchy *Amerikanka* for the hell of it. Who knows, maybe I would slide some dollars their way.

I was betting these boys had tired of their little charade and were perhaps a bit sorry to be picking on a woman old enough to have been their mother, so I picked up my purse, slung it over my shoulder, and walked out. Laurie and Mike were waiting outside the shed, and we got on the train without looking back. The guards had lost interest in us.

The men told me that absolutely nothing happened while we were separated. "The guards just futzed around," Mike said. "They seemed to be totally bumfuzzled."

The train lurched forward almost as soon as we got on, and we were on our way again. Tallinn never looked so beautiful as it did that June morning.

Imbi knew we'd only have the day since we had to get back to Moscow on the night train to catch our flight home. After lots of hugs and telling the story of our "interrogation," she was bursting with some news to share.

"You should know that you've come on a very important day. Today the money changes! Today no business can accept rubles any more, only Estonian kroons."

She was beaming at the idea of such a significant step on the road to Estonia's new democracy, and we weren't particularly bothered. Although we had wallets full of rubles, we also had dollars, and we'd rarely had trouble changing them to any local currency.

We're starved, so let's find a restaurant, and we can change money on the way.

Uh, not this time!

Not a single exchange was prepared to trade dollars for kroons. They said they had to save all the new currency for citizens bringing in rubles. Would they change our rubles? No, residents of Tallinn only (and Imbi already had her documents stamped with an exchange).

Imbi had only a few kroons with her, and a train trip out to her home on the edge of the city and back would have taken a big chunk out of the few hours we had. We tried restaurant after restaurant, waving dollars like greedy Yanks, but were told over and over that it was too risky, with officials watching everywhere, on the Day the Money Changed.

Finally, we took the elevator to the top-floor restaurant at the pricey Hotel Viru. If any business would take dollars anywhere, this was the place.

Dollars? No, so sorry.

In a moment of pure desperation, I asked, *Kreditnaya karta?*

We take only Visa! Sweeter words I'd never heard. We sat down to eat for the first time in nearly twenty-four hours, with plans to write the credit card company with the theme for a perfect commercial: When they won't take dollars, they'll take Visa!

Plastic trumped greenbacks on the Day the Money Changed!

I HAD PLENTY of time to let my thoughts wander on the way to the airport that April morning. Besides being quiet, Gennady had chosen a longer route following the river instead of taking Leningradskiy Prospekt, which had a few hills to climb. I smirked as I recalled one of those ever-popular jokes about Ladas and their long-suffering owners.

What do you call a Lada on the top of a hill? A miracle!

What do you call a Lada owner who says he got a speeding ticket? A liar!

Sorry, I couldn't resist.

But Gennady's yellow Lada got me to Sheremetyevo in plenty of time for the 7 a.m. Lufthansa flight to Frankfurt and then on the 10 a.m. non-stop to San Francisco. I'd be home by 12:30 p.m. that same Saturday after sixteen hours of travel. Making that ten o'clock flight from Frankfurt made the whole itinerary work, so I had left nothing to chance the day before. I repeated the steps I'd taken a month earlier when I had picked up my tickets—two buses, the Metro, and a hike across a muddy construction site next to *Olimpiyskiy Stadion* (Olympic Stadium—the main venue of the 1980 Olympics which the United States boycotted) to the Lufthansa office. It took another half an hour after I got there, but I was able to confirm my seats on both flights and pick up my boarding passes.

Couldn't I have done that on the phone and saved myself the trip? Maybe, but it was more than eagerness to be home that was driving me right now. I wanted to see a doctor, my doctor, about some odd symptoms I'd been experiencing off and on for nearly a month. Twice I'd awakened in the middle of night with chest pain, and the first time I was sure I was having a heart attack.

Terrific. Preserving my health in Russia was Job One for me. I brought amoxicillin, Monistat for yeast infections, Tums, Tylenol, Imodium, even some weird gel that was supposed to alleviate the pain of a toothache—and a paperback book of natural health remedies. I may have been living a fairly Russian life during my stay, but I did not want to see the inside of a Moscow polyclinic as a patient (despite the presence of one just a half-block from my apartment).

I used to joke about my personal *apteka* (pharmacy) that I carried on every trip. Besides the usual *medikamenty,* I had a package of disposable syringes in my purse at all times. Syringes had been in short supply in much of the former Soviet Union, and I didn't want to take a chance on needing an injection with a re-used one. My doctor had written a prescription for syringes to convince nosy Customs inspectors that they were a medical necessity.

I also had the twenty-four hour telephone number of the American Clinic in Moscow, in which USIA had enrolled me, as well as evacuation insurance that would allow me to be transported to Helsinki in an emergency—although I wasn't quite sure what constituted an emergency. Would they let me make that call?

That scary night, I wrapped myself in my down comforter and crawled out of bed. I had taped the clinic phone number (printed in huge block characters so I could read it without my glasses) on the table next to the phone. But when I stood up to turn on the light, I could feel the knot in my chest relaxing. I took some deep breaths and let the panic subside a bit. Then I dialed the number on that red toy phone.

Someone answered almost immediately (yes!) but I could barely hear him/her. It appeared that I could be heard, though, so I plunged ahead with a description of my symptoms, completely aware that I was probably talking to a clerk. I said I couldn't hear much.

What I could make out from the response told me that I was talking to a doctor (female, I think) and she was asking if I'd ever suffered from heartburn? No, never. I had all kinds of gut problems (ulcerative colitis the most serious) most of my life but heartburn wasn't one of them.

I chattered on for another minute or so before I realized that the line was dead—and I was not!

Heartburn, of all things! I found the paperback health manual and located the entry on heartburn. It really did sound as if it fit the symptoms. I dug through the box that served as my medicine cabinet for my bottle of Tums, popped a handful, and went back to bed.

The next time it happened, I was ready. No panic—just annoyance at having my sleep interrupted. But that wasn't the end of the weirdness. On April Fools' Day, the unofficial first day of spring in Moscow when women pack away their furs and bring out their pastel wool coats and hats, regardless of the temperature or other weather conditions, I fainted.

Luckily I was in my tiny office, just starting my Mr. Rogers morning routine (boots and leggings off, heels and nylons on), and I just slid down the wall to the floor. The room wasn't big enough for me to actually fall. Next thing I remember, the *dezhurnaya* from the front desk, was slapping my cheeks and wiping my face with a cold, damp, reasonably clean cloth. She clucked after me for a few minutes and then left me to drink some tea at my desk. As far as I could tell, she never mentioned the episode to a soul, despite the fact that I was a most inviting target for office gossip.

The last time I could remember fainting was at Yosemite National Park when I was newly pregnant with Robyn, roughly twenty-six years before. Sipping my tea (no sugar cubes or jam, thank you!), I mulled the link between my two fainting episodes. The conclusion was obvious: My reproductive system was in the throes of change! I knew I wasn't pregnant this time so it was probably the other one, the big one—and at age fifty, I was no doubt due.

So I would pay Dr. Reynolds a visit while I was at home. He had been through a lot with our family. I was referred to him just a few months after Laurie and I moved to San Mateo shortly after our abbreviated January 1967 wedding during the Snowstorm of the Century in Chicago.

Thirteen guests, out of the hundred or so invited, had made it to the church through the snowdrifts (after I helped shovel the sidewalk in my wedding gown). My bouquet was a couple of plastic glamellias since the florist could get no fresh flowers, and the cake was frozen since the baker was sure no one was getting married on this Saturday.

But we did.

When we arrived at the Palmer House Hotel downtown where we had reservations for our wedding night, we found the lobby full of people sleeping on couches and chairs, who were stranded in the city—and no room for us. When the desk clerk burst out laughing at our predicament, a man standing nearby, a true romantic, tossed his key across the counter and said, "Give them mine!" He even ordered champagne!

The next morning, we were out of town as soon as we could locate my 1960 Mercury Comet in the snow banks of Evanston and find a passing tow truck to jump-start the battery. It took six hours to go about thirty miles across the snow-shocked city to my folks' house where my mother had hung my ivory velvet wedding gown over the fireplace—sort of a shrine to the wedding that might have been. We packed up and headed west (well, first south and then west).

We stopped in Kansas City, where Laurie had grown up and where I had been working at the *Kansas City Star*, to pick up some of my things, and then we headed to California, stopping every night when the brushes in the generator of the Comet failed, and we had to get replacements. The car lasted just long enough to get us to San Francisco.

Laurie started work at Del Monte Corporation as a management trainee just three days after we found our first flat near Golden Gate Park in San Francisco, and I started at the Hearst-owned *San Francisco Examiner* the following week. But Laurie was much more nervous about starting his job than I expected. He had interviewed with Del Monte recruiters while he was finishing his statistics degree at the University of Missouri in Columbia. He'd taken a whole battery of tests and had just gotten the job offer when he called me in Kansas City where I was rooming with a high school friend of his and working at *The Star*.

"How would you like to live in San Francisco?"

I blanked for a moment while my universe shifted. He'd been planning to start law school at U.M. Kansas City in the spring and follow his dad into a career in law. That's why I took the job in Kansas City. But I'd grown up in Escondido in Southern California, near San Diego, and getting back to California struck a chord.

"Yes! It's as if you said, would I like to live in Valhalla? Yes! Let's do it!"

It wasn't until later that he told me he'd decided some time ago he would have made a lousy lawyer and working with his dad didn't hold much appeal. But he didn't know how to tell me. Maybe I wanted to marry a lawyer instead of a management trainee at Del Monte.

The hard part wasn't starting new in San Francisco; it was leaving *The Star* where I was thriving. I'd started as a copyeditor in July after I collected my Bachelor of Journalism degree at Mizzou's School of Journalism. This was the Golden Age of newspapering, and I had a couple of job offers—one with Associated Press in Moscow (where I could put six years of Russian language study to good use) and one at the *Rome American* where, well, where it was Rome!

But Laurie was going to law school in Kansas City, and I answered when *The Star* called. Metropolitan newspapering was still largely a man's world, but the editor had a modesty panel installed on one of the desks around the rim of the copy desk, and I became one of the guys! However, the guys were mostly rumpled and worn-out beat reporters (think *Front Page*) who weren't enthusiastic about taking the "slot," the copy chief's spot, on Saturday nights to lay out Sunday's paper. So, less than a month on the job, I moved into the slot on Saturday nights and directed the production of the Sunday edition of a 350,000-circulation daily newspaper that served four states. I was in Heaven!

Those late Saturday nights had one huge benefit: About 11 p.m. a delivery man from Arthur Bryant's Barbecue showed up with a massive spread of chicken and ribs, and we smeared Bryant's prize-winning barbecue sauce all over the page proofs as we worked. I never knew who paid for the feast, but it was splendid.

I'd generally wrap up about 2 a.m. and rouse a sleeping copy boy to walk me to my car. Nobody else got a late-night escort, but I figured I'd earned it.

I hated having to tell the managing editor that I was leaving after the opportunities *The Star* had offered me, but he just shrugged and said he'd be happy to help me get a job in San Francisco. In fact he called Bill German, his counterpart at *The Examiner*, and, before I knew it, I had a job waiting in San Francisco.

But not for long.

Just ten days after I set up my desk in the newsroom of *The Examiner*, German called me into his office and told me that the merger of the *San Francisco Call Bulletin* with *The Examiner* had finalized, and he was required to absorb as many of the *Call Bulletin* staff members as he could. The Newspaper Guild contract was clear: Last hired, first fired. That, uh, was me.

German handed me a AAA map with a San Mateo intersection circled on it and the keys to his car. *The San Mateo Times* has an opening, he said, and they're expecting you.

The Times did have an opening, but it was for a Lifestyle reporter, far removed from the buzz of the newsroom that I'd enjoyed at *The Star* and far more gender-typed than I had hoped for. I interviewed with the managing editor George Whitesell, who chewed on an unlit cigar while we talked.

"What are my chances of getting into the newsroom?" I asked.

"Not a snowball's chance in hell. I've already got my broad!"

I took the job in the Lifestyle section (and made a lifelong friend of the editor Mary Jane Clinton), but in 1988 I slid into Whitesell's slot as managing editor of *The Times,* one of only three female editors of daily newspapers in California.

He kept the cigar.

As it turned out, the twelve years I spent as a feature writer (and sewing columnist!) in Lifestyle allowed me the freedom to work part-time until Robyn and then David were in school all day. Careers for women with those opportunities were hard to come by in the seventies but, after I returned to *The Times* full time, I was itching to get back in the newsroom.

The assassination attempt on President Reagan in 1981 provided my entree. The bells on the teletype machines started chiming about noon on March 30, and the newsroom was deserted. At that hour, *The Times* was between the three-star and four-star or final editions, and the staff routinely disappeared for lunch during that break. The paper had recently adopted a new computerized pagination and production system, which had effectively replaced the Associated Press teletype machines, a staple of newspapering in the first half of the twentieth century. But they were still clattering along at *The Times,* and the bells meant something big.

I jumped up and ran to read the yellow tape reeling out just as the current managing editor, Virgil Wilson, came out of the backshop.

WASHINGTON (AP) — President Ronald Reagan was shot outside the Hilton Hotel at 2:27 p.m. (EST). Condition unknown.

That was all we had, but AP would send updates every minute or so. Virgil turned to me. "I'll call the press room to hold for a replate, but I don't know how to use the new system. Do you?"

I did. Not only that, I'd done this drill a dozen times at *The Star.*

I sat down at a monitor in the newsroom, opened the AP folder on the screen and started meshing a few brief paragraphs together. That's all we'd have room for as we'd trim the stories already on Page One and push them down to make room for a three-inch strip across the top above the nameplate.

Virgil pulled the compositors (all men at that time) out of the lunchroom to remake Page One and the jump page. I built the story and wrote the headline PRESIDENT REAGAN SHOT in end-of-the-world block type. Then I opened the pagination system and redesigned Page One with the story and head. Within eight minutes, the actual photographic paper that would be affixed to the composition board of Page One of the replated three-star edition slid out of the printer in the backshop.

While Virgil stood over the compositor, directing where to cut the stories already on the page and how far to move everything down, I was reshaping the lead graph and writing a sub-head: "Press Secretary Brady gravely injured in attack." As other staffers rushed back in after hearing the news on the radio, they picked up other tasks, downloading the first photos of the assassination attempt and reshaping other stories to make the lead story fit.

By the time the Final was off the floor around 2 p.m., I'd rewritten the story from AP blasts at least six times, including two that reported that Jim Brady was dead. The last one had Brady clinging to life and Reagan in surgery, and that would be the edition that landed on the doorsteps of the core of our circulation area that afternoon.

The adrenaline was still pumping when Virgil stopped at the computer where I'd been for the past two hours and called me in to his office.

"I want you in the newsroom. We'll have to shift things around in here and come up with an appropriate title, but wrap up what you're working on in Lifestyle. I'll talk to Mary Jane."

The title was deputy news editor, and I would lay out the main news section of *The Times* every day from then on.

I was over the moon! And Laurie shared my joy in his low-key way. He brought me flowers and designed a plan to get the kids (now eight and eleven) off to school in the morning, now that I would be starting work at five thirty each morning (the curse of afternoon newspapers). Since he would have to leave for the train before they left, he put an alarm clock on the kitchen counter, set for the time they needed to leave for the short walk to school. I would now be finished with my workday in time to pick them up and get them to after-school activities.

President Reagan figured in another bright spot in my newspaper career. In 1983, nearly two hundred and fifty Americans were killed when the Marine barracks in Beirut was attacked during the Lebanese civil war. Reagan was under pressure to remove all the Americans from the war zone but, just before the *The Times'* four-star deadline, he announced that the troops would stay. I remade the page with a one-column sidebar that dropped out of the main story on the fighting in Beirut. One-column heads give you very little space for nuance, but I was sure I'd caught the gist of the story well with:

Reagan
firm on
pullout

I noticed some backshop snickering as the page went to press, but it wasn't until Laurie guffawed at the dinner table that I realized what

I'd done. And my *faux pas* didn't escape the notice of Herb Caen, the celebrated columnist of *The San Francisco Chronicle* who repeated it for the entire Bay Area to enjoy. The headline was the highlight of my retirement roast!

THOSE SIXTEEN HOURS of travel offered lots of time for reflection, but by early afternoon I pushed my way through the double doors of Customs at SFO, and there was Laurie! I could see him before he saw me. I had my camera out and snapped a photo of him holding flowers and rocking back on his heels as he always did while waiting. I'd forgotten that. (What else had I forgotten?)

He also had added a little bit of a paunch that I blamed on too many fast-food meals while I was gone. I was ticking off a mental list of the high cost Laurie was paying for my Great Adventure.

And then I was in his arms, and I burrowed into the comfort of his size and that bear hug that could wrap up my five-foot-eight frame—and the lingering kiss. Everything would be all right.

The next ten days seemed to move at fast-forward, and I was stunned when Laurie said he would have to be in Stockton at least a few of the days I was home because the warehouse automation project was finally beginning to jell. But he would be home every evening even if it meant ninety-minute commutes each way.

David came home from UC Santa Barbara on Monday, and we had time to talk. He'd wrestled with depression at school and had found real value in therapy sessions with a psychologist. He was the introspective one of my kids, and I valued his observations. I'd asked him in an e-mail how his dad was doing.

"He's pretty miserable by himself," he'd replied, "and I think that project is eating him alive, but you're the only person Dad is ever honest with about his feelings. I've heard him tell people he misses you, and it will be a rough time for him, which are reflections of his love for you, but as for his actual internal feelings, like 'I'm scared' or 'I'll be lonely,' never. The world is yours. And as long as the world is yours, the world is all right with him.

"You've said that Dad is egoless, and I believe this is true. But it's not an asset. Humility, modesty, reliability, innocence—these are his assets. But the lack of ego is a lack of self and, without self, you can't really know yourself or reveal anything of yourself."

Robyn had seen the most of Laurie while I was gone. They both had made an effort to spend time together every couple of weeks, usually in San Francisco where she was living with her boyfriend and teaching pre-school. She agreed with David's assessment.

"But I don't think he's really depressed. He just doesn't know what to do with himself with you gone."

I was worried enough to ask Laurie one night as we talked in bed if he thought I should throw in the towel and stay home.

"You can't." He bolted upright. "You made a commitment, and you can't just back out because you're homesick. And you can't use me as an excuse! I'm down because of this project, and I would still be down if you were home.

"Besides, you got that grant in a lump sum in January, and you'd have to give it back if you didn't see it through."

I have no doubt he meant exactly what he said. We had been embroiled in an ongoing exchange of letters and phone calls with Blue Cross a few years earlier when our overlapping health plans both reimbursed us for a bill for hospital tests. He returned the check to Blue Cross—and they issued another one. This went on for months until we got a phone call from a vice president at Blue Cross asking us to please cash the check and donate it to a good cause since their computer system wasn't set up to accept returned checks.

This same stubborn honesty was giving him fits as he tried to figure out how we would pay income tax on my grant since part of it was a *per diem* for living expenses. He made an appointment for us to talk to a tax consultant in San Francisco while I was home since he couldn't get a satisfactory answer from the IRS.

He'd also wanted to know if I needed to pay income tax in Russia so I had asked Svet for advice on where I could get a definitive answer. He laughed.

Such a funny question! Russians never pay taxes unless someone comes and tells them they have to pay or go to prison!

He was right. Most Russians I talked to considered tax avoidance as something of a patriotic duty. The government should try to collect taxes from the *biznesmen* and leave them alone.

I posed the question to my new handler at USIA, Valerie Kreutzer, and Laurie was finally satisfied when she sent an "official" response: No need to file anything in Russia.

So it was settled that I was going back, but I planned to broach Laurie's blue moods with Dr. Reynolds, who had seen us through a lot over the past twenty-eight years. He diagnosed my colitis not long after we moved to Belmont on the San Francisco Peninsula in May 1967. He sent me home from our first consultation with three medical books with the references marked. This was a chronic condition, he said, and those articles would give me a good idea of how I could manage it. I liked his directness.

He delivered both children—or "caught" them as he said, in reference to the fact that I barely made it to the hospital in time to deliver with both of them. ("You could drive a Mack truck through there" was his blunt assessment of my birth canal during my first pregnancy visit!) At one of my early well-baby visits with Robyn, he suggested that I really ought to think about going back to work—advice not many young mothers could expect to hear from their doctors in the seventies, but music to my ears.

Later he guided us through Robyn's childhood medical crisis, a congenital defect in her urinary tract, even though we were by then seeing specialists and surgeons as well. In fact, he was the one who suggested a pediatric nephrologist in San Francisco who finally helped solve the issue after seven failed surgeries.

He also stood by Laurie and me as we fought the hospital for the right to spend the night with Robyn when she was hospitalized. I wrote a series on the issue for *The Times* that eventually led to a change in hospital policy.

So, what was the matter with me now? He asked about my symptoms: Hot flashes? No. Fatigue? Nope. Sleeplessness? Not likely, I still slept like the dead most nights. But after an exam, he confirmed my suspicion.

"Menopause, yes, but it sounds as if you may get a pass on the worst of it. I think that's only fair after your history with menstrual pain."

Then I asked him about Laurie. As I expected, he said there were mild medications that might help, and he could suggest a psychologist but he would need to talk to Laurie first. I didn't think that was likely to happen, but Laurie was interested to hear about my diagnosis.

Guess you can't get pregnant now! He was sniggering—just like a man!

He did get a kick out of going with me to buy mesh screening for those tall casement windows of my Moscow flat. Warm weather was coming with the longer days, and so were the mosquitoes! On more than one trip to Russia, I had sweltered through hot and humid nights because opening the windows would let the bugs in. I've always been especially tasty to biting insects, and Russian mosquitoes found me particularly exotic.

On April 1, my *hozayka* (landlady) had left a telephone message: Michelle, it is time to open the windows and door to the balcony so you can feel the breeze from the river. Pull the tape away very gently, please. The drapes will keep the mosquitoes out.

Not likely. I'd removed those orange sateen drapes months ago and folded them away until the day I would pack up to go home, and I knew no self-respecting Moscow mosquito would be deterred by them anyway. A canister vacuum cleaner, I was told by the ex-pat kids in the RAPIC office, was the weapon of choice to suck up the mosquitoes I could expect to blanket my inside walls.

No, I would bring back proper window screening (to be secured by thumbtacks or a staple gun, if I could find one) and a summer's supply of Off.

And in an instant it was time to go back. But not before Laurie showed me a memo he'd written to the supervisor of the Del Monte project. He would be taking the first two weeks of September away from the project so he could go to Barcelona with me and then back to Moscow.

"If the project's done, I'll stay until you come home."

Letters From Russia
What am I doing over here?

MOSCOW — A Letter to the Editor writer to *The Times* wants to know what I'm doing over here besides slipping on the ice and dealing with broken locks. He wants to know what a "journalist-in-residence" actually does in Russia, considering that my support comes from American taxpayers through the United States Information Agency.

Fair enough. What am I doing here?

In short, I'm serving as both midwife and godmother at the birth of a free press. The midwife part involves dealing with the desperate survival crises of newly independent newspapers which, for the first time, are having to make ends meet without the benefit of government or party subsidies. That means attracting advertising to pay most of the bills, learning marketing and promotion techniques to position themselves in a crowded market (there are eighty newspapers in Moscow alone) and locking in a committed and enthusiastic readership.

My most recent role as managing editor of *The Times* prepared me better than most editors to talk about the survival issues with Russian newspaper editors. Even though I've spent my professional career on the news side of newspapers, a managing editor at a mid-sized daily in the US is well tuned in to what's going on in all the other departments of the paper. Russian editors, however, don't have the benefit of our clear separation of editorial and advertising functions, and the blurring of those functions creates some of the most difficult ethical and philosophical issues that the godmother part of me has to tangle with.

The largest part of my time here is spent helping Russian editors forge strong links with their readership through effective newsroom management and user-friendly newspaper design. I do this through seminars for newspaper editors in Moscow and throughout the cities of Russia's eleven time zones.

The Russian American Press and Information Center in Moscow (where I have an office) uses its press connections in the regions to announce my seminars and work out the logistics of my travel. The seminars are well-received. In every city, we've had to add at least one and sometimes as many as three to the schedule to accommodate the number who want to attend.

I give a portion of the seminar in Russian and the rest in English with the help of an interpreter—although the editors and I all speak a third language, newspapers. I encourage lots of interaction and discussion and require participants to bring their newspapers, which I critique and use as examples.

The content of the seminars changes with each city I visit as I learn more from the editors and gather more Russian examples of good design work that I can share with the editors at the next stop. I've started getting feedback from the cities I've visited earlier, and it feels terrific. Two young editors in Khabarovsk in the Russian Far East just sent me three editions of a special insert they are now doing on computers. They were attractively designed and chockful of advertising. The editors already had the idea of doing the insert when we met, but they said my encouragement, suggestions and gentle prodding of the editor-in-chief got the project moving.

Every seminar heads in a different direction, and I follow where the editors want to go. It usually ends up with a discussion about First Amendment issues, press law and journalistic ethics—a hot topic in a country where editors are just learning that freedom of the press includes the freedom to go out of business. Over and over, I've heard that ethics are something Russian newspapers can't yet afford.

Remarkably, they are interested and eager to hear what I have to say. I carefully avoid preaching and the "you people should" speech that I hear often enough around here. There's no reason to assume that Russian newspapers should adopt the American newspaper model; no other country in the world has replicated the American system so why should Russia. I tell editors that I am offering some ideas that work in the U.S. and sharing ideas that I've found working well in Russian newspapers, and I hope they'll find one or two that will work for them.

Are those American taxpayers (of which I'm one) getting their money's worth? Only if you believe that nurturing the growth of a free and robust press in this rapidly changing country is in the best interest of the United States.

Obviously I do—and I've bet a year of my professional life on it.

Chapter Eight

THE MOSCOW I returned to was not the Moscow I'd left.

In just two weeks, the blackened, eroded snow stacks and grimy pools of oily sludge that defined spring in Russia had vanished. The bone-bare cottonwood trees that lined the embankment below my apartment windows had morphed into bright green billows. No longer could I watch the Great Dane that lived in the flat above me (known as Dawg) try to run between the tree trunks with a three-foot stick in his mouth—only to go somersaulting when the stick stuck. Now Dawg was lost in the leafiness below me (although I could always hear him thumping down the stairs).

The river's ice floes had been replaced with barges (mysteriously loaded with sand and going in *both* directions) and sightseeing boats. The far bank had sprouted picnic tables and brightly striped canopies for the concessionaires setting up shop. On my side of the river, young *biznesmen* had rigged lines over the concrete wall to haul up buckets of water for their car-washing operations. Ladas and limos alike blocked traffic to get in line.

Everything was bright and clean, and I marveled in the moment. I had spent many hot and limp summer days in Moscow during past visits, but these balmy 25-degree C days buoyed me.

I'd been on shaky ground, with tears threatening, ever since I'd kissed Laurie good-bye at San Francisco International. My overnight debriefing stop in Washington, D.C. hadn't helped much, although I did face the fact that I was glad I wouldn't have to tell Valerie that I wasn't going back. I *did* want to go back, not just because I'd made a promise, but because this year was shape-shifting into something very good.

My show-and-tells were SRO, and follow-up invitations to spend time at local newspapers poured in after each one. I was feeling a little like Sally Field at the Oscars ("You *do* like me!") and my comfort level at RAPIC and on the road was on the rise.

What's more, I'd learned that I could do this. I could make it by myself half a planet from home in a not-quite-so foreign culture, and I was having fun. I hated that I wasn't there for Laurie when he so clearly needed support but, perhaps for the first time since I arrived, I knew this Great Adventure business was working out.

But I did feel guilty, especially at night.

For my Washington debrief, Valerie had pulled a group of Russia specialists from a number of federal agencies together to listen and ask questions as I reported on the first half (almost) of my tour of duty. I needed written materials in Russian that I could leave with the editors I worked with, I told them, and offered to create a newspaper design manual in the months I had left.

Valerie mentioned a couple of funding sources that she could tap for the cost if I could write it. I could do better than that; I could write it, translate it (with the help of good friend—and superb linguist—Tatiana Patina), and lay it out in PageMaker to create a camera-ready copy.

I'd discovered that PageMaker, software that combines text and images on a page, was the go-to software in Russia for producing newspapers of every size and every taste. It was almost always pirated, but I'd come by my new updated version honestly.

In fact, I could claim to be something of a PageMaker pioneer. While both Robyn and David were at Hillsdale High School in San Mateo, I had volunteered to work with their student newspaper. My afternoons were free, so I started mother-henning *The Scroll* at Hillsdale in the mid-eighties (although my kids, both excellent writers, wouldn't come anywhere near).

During the summer after my first year, I got a phone call from the principal asking me to come to a meeting with some people from Apple Computer. They had quite an offer: They would outfit *The Scroll* with Macintosh desktop computers and a LaserWriter printer if we (that would be me) agreed to be a beta test site for a new software program called PageMaker to lay out the paper.

Did they notice that I was drooling at the offer? Yes, I would do it! Absolutely!

Laurie was as intrigued as I was when I told him about it. The computers he used at Del Monte filled entire floors of the skyscraper, but he was convinced that the potential of desktop computing had barely been tapped. He wanted to play with this new toy as much as I did, so we used my new "educator" Apple discount to buy our own Macintosh Plus.

Apple was as good as its word. Eight Macs were installed along with a LaserWriter, which was pretty hefty at the time. I wangled two days off from *The Times* for training at the Apple offices in Cupertino, a few miles south of San Mateo in what would soon be known as Silicon Valley, to learn how to use PageMaker.

Why was I so big on this? I was looking a long way past *The Scroll* to the broader uses of similar systems at *The Times* (although the tech people at *The Times* were nothing more than annoyed at all my cheery chatter about the possibilities). Apple was proposing to create a way for newspapers or magazines (or anything using ink and paper) to produce its pages camera-ready for the printer. No more galleys of lead type, no more lead photo engravings, and no more through-the-roof costs. This system would be called Desktop Publishing, and I was a midwife at the birth!

It's no surprise that teenagers were the first to grasp this totally new technology, and my journalism junkies were as thrilled as I was. The staff doubled that first year as word got around, and Laurie signed on as tech support to solve our production-night snafus. For the cherry on the sundae, *Newsweek* magazine did a story on the first high school newspaper produced with Desktop Publishing—and we were it!

My first registration number for PageMaker reflected *The Scroll's* beta status—just six digits. From then on, every time I registered an update, I had to type in a string of zeros at the beginning of the number to make it work—just as I had for the stack of floppy disks holding the latest version of PageMaker that I packed back to Russia that spring.

MOSCOW SPARKLED FOR still another reason that first week in May. President Bill Clinton was coming to celebrate the fiftieth anniversary of Victory Day, the end of the Great Patriotic War on May 9. (I know, Europe observes May 8 as the end of the war on the Continent, but Russia, for reasons known only to Russia, prefers May 9.)

The local press tsk-tsked that Clinton wouldn't attend the displays of military hardware that were traditional on Victory Day— as an expression of America's pique with Russia's war against its own people in Chechnya. But he would "bless" the newly opened Victory Park on Poklonnaya Hill and address World War II veterans and the relatives of the twenty-six million Russians who died in the war. He admitted that the recently thawed Cold War had "obscured our ability to fully appreciate what your people had suffered and how your extraordinary courage helped to hasten the victory we all celebrate today."

I leaned out from my balcony railing to watch Clinton's motorcade arrive at the Russian White House, which I could see from my flat. Laurie and I had met the President the year before at an American Society of Newspaper Editors reception. We were both blown away by his ability to remember our names and newspapers and personal minutiae. As we shook hands in the reception line, I said I was pleased to see that he and the First Lady had visited the Katyn Memorial near Minsk in a recent trip to Belarus. Laurie added that he should read my book about the aftermath of Chernobyl.

"Yes, *Children of Chernobyl*," Clinton didn't blink. "They gave us a copy in Minsk, and it's on Hillary's bedside table."

But it wasn't Clinton's memory that had people in Moscow gaping; it was his shorts, his very short, running shorts which he wore for his morning jog along the Moscow River. Not very dignified for a president, my neighbor sniffed as we watched from our balconies.

After an extraordinarily hot May (ten straight days in the eighties and nineties), the cottonwood trees were taking their June revenge. The air was full of little puffs of white fluff that look much like dandelions in their post-blossom stage. Russians call the puffs *pukh*, the perfect word for all sorts of unnamed mysteries of life—the gunk that accumulates in the corners of pockets, bellybutton lint, dust balls behind the refrigerator, clouds of dog and cat hair, that sort of thing.

For a few weeks in late spring each year, *pukh* rains and reigns in Russia. It accumulates on window screens, if you're lucky enough to have them, or all over everything in your flat if you're not. Laundry hanging on the rack on the balcony looks as if it's grown mold by the time it's dry.

I don't need to tell you what *pukh* means if you have allergies—like an acacia tree growing outside your bedroom window. Most Muscovites don't seem to suffer *pukh* attacks—other than having to pluck *pukh* out of their ice cream cones and off their clothes. But Americans suffered mightily. If you saw someone walking through a *pukh* cloud with handkerchief at the ready, eyes red and nose running, you're just about guaranteed to hear him or her speak with the broad vowels and rounded consonants of American English.

Word had it that this year's early onslaught of *pukh* forced Clinton to limit his jogging to the morning only. Clinton staff members blamed his heavy-lidded lethargy at official sessions on an allergy attack. Local ex-pats nodded in sympathy, recognizing the effects of preseasonal *pukh*.

LAURIE HAD GREAT news when he called that week. The warehouse project had leapt ahead when he tweaked the "wands" that the forklifts used to read the UPC codes. He was thrilled!

"We know it will work now. We know this is the way to go. Guess I fooled 'em again!"

He just couldn't shake that disbelief in his own worth—even when he was celebrating that very thing.

He ran through a list of smaller issues to deal with, but Del Monte was satisfied that this was the system they would adopt for the warehouse in Stockton and, they expected, all their warehouses across the country. Laurie joked that he'd be going back to his roots. He'd been born in Salina, Kansas, and Del Monte wanted to install the system in Topeka, Kansas, next. He must have heard me gasp; I surely wasn't ready for another long separation so soon after this one.

"But not 'till next year, for sure. I've told them I'm coming back with you in September. They know all about it."

Now that he could take a breath, he wanted to get a group of friends together at the cabin during the summer. Our cabin in Long Barn in the central Sierra Nevada above Yosemite had been at the core of our family life for more than twenty years. But only Laurie's scrupulous (some might say "tight") budgeting allowed us to have it in the first place.

Just one year after we bought our house on Thirty-ninth Avenue in San Mateo, Laurie looked up from paying bills at his desk to say that he was pretty sure we could buy a cabin in the Sierra this year if we could find one for the right price. I shot back: How could we afford a cabin? We just took out a forty-thousand-dollar mortgage for a house!

But we could, he showed me, if we weren't too picky.

We started looking around the Dodge Ridge Ski Area where we had both learned to ski in the first year of our marriage. We loved the low-key, "un-touristy" atmosphere of the region, and we could get there from home in three hours instead of the four *or more* to Lake Tahoe. We packed the kids in the car several winter weekends and trudged through the knee-high snowdrifts to look at what was available in our price range—which was not much.

On one trip in March, I stayed with the kids (both with fevers and coughs) in our rented cabin while Laurie went out with a realtor to look. He was gone less than an hour when he came back for me so I could go with the realtor. He'd found a real possibility, but he whispered to me on the way out, "Don't want it too much. I think we can get it for less than they're asking."

I didn't want it at all!

Apparently the former owners had split up and just walked away—with the refrigerator full of rotting food, piles of mildewed clothes in the closets, mice turds in the dresser drawers, and layer upon layer of stink. Laurie argued (and we did argue!) that everything was fixable. Structurally it was sound and winterized, and he'd already come up with a low-ball offer, no doubt the only offer. They jumped at it, and we had our vacation cabin—such as it was.

The arguing didn't end there, and I rarely fight fair. While others whine or yell or throw things, I sink into smoldering silence. Laurie explained; I smirked. And all for nothing! I had signed the papers, and that redwood A-frame at the edge of the national forest was already ours.

Major elbow grease and untold trips to the dump eventually proved Laurie's logic. It turned out to be a great getaway spot that stamped itself on our family, especially our children (Robyn, five, and David, two, at the time). Over the next twenty years, the Carter cabin had hosted winter ski gatherings and summer trips to Pinecrest Lake and all the forks of the Stanislaus and Tuolumne Rivers near us. Family albums are stuffed with photos of our kids and our friends' kids splashing in mountain streams, hiking dusty trails, and tobogganing down the snow-packed slope behind the house.

I had always done the organizing of cabin get-togethers, so Laurie asked what to do first. He'd already decided it would be a weekend in July, and I suggested he poll friends to agree on a date and then assign different meals to different couples.

"That really sounds like more planning than I want to do," he said. "I'm thinking of telling people to bring whatever they want. It'll be a Zen weekend."

Not my way of doing it, but it was his trip. I was just thrilled that he was eager to be surrounded by friends at a place that had meant so much to him over the years.

"Oh, by the way," he added, "look for a surprise this week!"

Flushed with his success with the anniversary roses, he wired a Mother's Day arrangement of carnations, daisies, and baby's breath *and* a box of Belgian chocolates this time. He created almost as much of a sensation at RAPIC as he had in January. The flowers came home with me that night, but the chocolates were gone after one pass through the office. Oh, well.

SVET WAS IN my office when I came in the next day, and he introduced me to the editor of the largest newspaper in Vladikavkaz in the southern republic of North Ossetia. Could I bring my seminar to the Caucasus in the next few weeks? That was one corner of Russia I'd never visited, and I had a little time before summer guests (including David) were due. Sure, why not.

Within a day or two, I knew why not: North Ossetia shared a border with the autonomous republic of Chechnya—which, at the moment, happened to be fighting a war of secession with Russia. Just spitting distance from rebel-held territory sat the city of Vladikavkaz.

The Press Office never intended to send me to the Caucasus because of the fighting and because the regional press office there had closed its doors nearly two years before. But the editor had heard me in Nizhny Novgorod in March and was sure he could pull together a group of newspaper editors from all over the Caucasus to make my trip worthwhile. He even had an excellent interpreter (another high school English teacher, sigh!) ready to help me.

Svet kept telling me that he would not pressure me to go while he called up an entire army to do just that. The RAPIC librarian Masha grew up in Vladikavkaz, and she brought in a shoebox full of photos. Soon my desk was stacked with leaflets, maps, and travel books about the Caucasus—and I caved.

Even the ever-adventurous twenty-something interns in the Press Office thought the trip was dicey at best. My landlady let me know that she thought I was absolutely mad. But I had come to Russia for a Great Adventure after all, (and I was eager to find out why I was considered Caucasian when I'd never even seen the Caucasus). Now was my chance.

I would travel alone this time since there was no regional RAPIC director, no Anna, to hold my hand. I'd fly to Mineralny Vody in southern Russia where a driver would pick me up and take me the rest of the way to Vladikavkaz by car. The flying part was always dodgy. The State Department (and airline pilot Mike) insisted that Americans not fly Aeroflot within Russia because of its dismal safety record, but the distances across Russia were so great (have I mentioned the eleven times zones!) that any other form of travel just didn't make sense. I could fly to Mineralny Vody in about two hours and fifteen minutes or I could take the train for thirty-three hours.

I would fly—as I had several other times this year.

FLYING IN RUSSIA always provided fodder for endless stories. I remember a flight to Novosibirsk on which I'd found a seat (with a working seatbelt and tray table!) next to a chatty businessman. Once we leveled off at cruise altitude, the cockpit door opened and a German shepherd trotted down the aisle. I turned to my seatmate: Did he know there was a dog in the cockpit?

"Of course! Don't you know the law?" He paused for effect. "There must always be someone sober in the cockpit."

He was thoroughly pleased with his joke and the rise it got out of me.

Another time I was waiting in Perm to board a flight back to Moscow, joining the scrum of passengers around the stairs at the back of an Antonov. In the midst of the jostling, a 2x4 plank, about two feet long, poked my arm. Why would anyone carry a 2x4 on the plane? Why, in fact, were many passengers packing planks? Should I have one too?

Once I was safely in my seat, the puzzle was solved. The boards were stretched across the center aisle to provide seats for far more people than this aircraft could safely carry. In an instant, I decided I didn't need to get back to Moscow all that much, but I couldn't have gotten out no matter how hard I tried. The aisle was blocked.

Nonetheless, I had survived the earlier ordeals, and this flight south to the Caucasus was uneventful as well, even if the three-and-a-half hour car ride was not. The journey, in pitch darkness, was punctuated every fifty miles or so by brightly lit and well-armed military checkpoints where the editor, the driver, and I handed over our passports for inspection. Clearly the presence of a middle-aged *Amerikanka* on the road to Vladikavkaz broke up an otherwise dull night for the guards since my *dokumenty* were passed around and debated at every stop.

Normal, all normal, the editor tried to assure me but, besides being scared witless, I really had to pee! However, you couldn't have paid me to leave the safety of the car and wander into the inky roadside darkness alone and squat behind a tree.

I was rather proud of my skill at peeing outside. I'd been on a lot of long car rides around Russia where rest stops with bathrooms were very few and far between. Men just stepped out of the car, turned their backs and unzipped; women, however, had to find a something to block the view. I could crouch quite comfortably with thighs together and ankles akimbo to avoid overspray. It was actually easier in the snow since the warm trickle melted into the crust instead of splashing. And I always had a quarter-roll of T.P. flattened in the bottom of my purse for just such occasion.

But this time, I suffered in silence.

THE EDITOR WAS as good as his word. The two daylong seminars were packed with journalists coming from as far as Georgia and Azerbaijan, and visits to several newspapers would fill out my week. But the real star of the adventure would be the Caucasus Mountains themselves, which stretch east-west between the Caspian and Black Seas, creating a wall between Europe and Asia in the south. With few foothills, they push nearly straight up off the flat steppes of southern Russian. Higher than the Alps, they define and dominate the region.

Vladikavkaz sits in the shadow of eighteen-thousand-foot Mount Elbrus, the highest peak in the range, and the seminar group decided a visit to Vladikavkaz was incomplete without an *ekskursiya* into the mountains. Our caravan consisted of two Ladas and a Moskvich, and not one of them looked up to the task. On a spectacularly warm, sunny day, we headed up, up, up, single-file with Oksana, the twelve-year-old daughter of the editor (who had studied a little English in school), as the tour guide.

One of the Ladas overheated about forty-five minutes into the climb, but we were prepared; the trunks of all the cars were loaded with jugs of water. We all piled out and picnicked in a vast meadow of wild flowers by the side of the road. While we waited for the car to cool down enough to add the water to the radiator, Oksana taught me how to braid a wild-flower wreath and insisted I wear one for the rest of the journey.

The next stop was planned. Our parade pulled to the side of the road near a broad overlook with only a stubby rock wall to keep us back from a shear drop of many thousand feet. Below us was a broad treeless plain that stretched as far as I could see.

Oksana had fallen asleep so her father handled the narration alone (getting louder and louder any time I didn't understand a phrase). This was the place where his people had watched their enemies approach for hundreds and hundreds of years.

Which enemies?

Genghis Khan!

I had been having trouble with his Russian dialect, but that I got! What an image it called up. I could see the open space below us alive with the Mongol horde on horseback, a vision fueled, no doubt, by those Hollywood mega-pics of my youth.

We climbed still further in the Moskvich, the only car that could handle the altitude; the rest of the party would wait for us at the overlook. About thirty minutes later, we bumped and jostled our way onto a rocky cleft in the side of the mountain well above the tree line. The editor's voice took on a reverent, subdued tone as he led me along a path into a series of half-collapsed chalk caves. This, he said, is the City of the Dead.

On shelves, carved into the walls, were row upon row of skeletons and mummified remains wrapped in scraps of ceremonial robes. The parents of my parents, he whispered. And many generations before that, I thought.

They were so small I asked if they were children. No, no, our parents.

The drive back to Vladikavkaz was quiet. Even Oksana, who had been non-stop chatter on the way up, understood the significance of this place and the honor they had shown me by bringing me there.

On the last day of my stay, they had promised me a party, but the weather was still so pleasant they decided on a *shashlik* barbecue at a favorite riverside spot. This involved another long drive, but the mostly level highway rambled alongside a small river with occasional rapids and one lovely waterfall.

Fire rings dotted the picnic site, and corncob coals were glowing when sticks were threaded with chunks of marinated sturgeon and balanced on rocks to grill. We sat on patterned rugs rolled out on the ground and ate until we groaned. It was the first time I'd eaten *shashlik* made from anything but lamb, but now I had a new favorite.

The vodka (and *shampanskoye* for me) was making the rounds after the meal when a single huge blast shattered the calm, and tracer fire shot across the early evening sky. Covered in dust, we sat in stunned silence for several seconds until one of the journalists piped up in perfect English: "Independence Day! Fireworks for you!"

The Fourth of July was still two weeks away. I appreciated the gesture, but it was time to get out of there. We were in the cars with pedals to the metal (which isn't all that fast in a Lada) just minutes before the next blast rippled the road behind us. It wasn't until we were safely back in Vladikavkaz that I learned our lovely riverside picnic site was actually in Chechnya!

So why am I considered to be Caucasian? I didn't find the answer in the Caucasus, but rather in a reference book in the RAPIC library: Because an eighteenth century anthropologist in Germany, who divided *homo sapiens* into five distinct races, thought the skull structure of the people in the Caucasus best represented his "white" grouping—and it stuck!

I COULDN'T GET on the Internet while I was in Vladikavkaz so my inbox was full when I got home. Laurie and David were knocking heads over a library book that the University of California at Santa Barbara said that David hadn't returned. The school was threatening to withhold his degree, which he had finished in May, over the cost of the book and some late charges. Laurie wanted David to find the book; David had moved out of his campus digs a month before and had no idea where the book was.

My shoulders slumped. We'd been happy to pay some five-digit sum for David's college education (even if daughter Robyn had refused our money and paid her own way through UC Santa Cruz). But now, after several phone calls, Laurie was thoroughly pissed with David over a forty-five-dollar book. I could only imagine how Laurie's own dad must have steamed when he found out he'd been writing tuition checks to the University of Missouri when Laurie wasn't even in school any more.

This was the second semester of Laurie's sophomore year at Missouri. He'd begun playing in all-night, booze-stoked bridge and poker marathons at the Sigma Chi house. Soon he'd quit going to class at all and, by spring break, MU's School of Engineering had told him not to come back in September. He'd convinced himself that he could talk his way back into school in the fall, but what he could *not* do was spend the summer at home listening to his parents rag on him. Instead, he took a job on a traveling team of college kids selling Great Books throughout the South. At his lowest point, he'd admitted to me, he even sold a set to a blind man.

In light of his own less-than-stellar college career, couldn't he cut David some slack over a forty-five-dollar library book? Please write the check, I sighed. He's starting a job in September, and he would need a clean transcript.

Laurie never mentioned it again, but he must have paid up or beaten UCSB into submission. All records show that David graduated—with a degree in art history. The previous summer Laurie had made it clear that he expected David to finish this year. David said he could complete a degree in math or black studies or art history—he had nearly enough credits in all three. Laurie's response was crisp: Pick one!

David, who finally had his visa for Russia, e-mailed from Washington, D.C., where he was visiting his girlfriend. He would arrive July 15.

Letters From Russia
Shopping in Russia requires newfound skills

MOSCOW — Shopping here is exhausting work, and just when I think I've got the hang of it, got a system all worked out, a new, purely Russian wrinkle surfaces to defeat me.

The interminable lines that were standard during the Soviet period are mostly gone. You may still have to queue up to buy bread but it's just a few minutes' wait; nothing like the block-long lines I saw here in the Eighties. And the store shelves are full—not often with things I want to buy—but full, nonetheless.

But the uniquely Russian system of buying groceries still baffles me. In all the neighborhood shops and most of the bigger *gastronomes*, every item you buy is an individual purchase involving three steps (and sometimes three queues). First, you select what you want ("Half a kilo of cheese, please.") The clerk cuts it and weighs it and tells you how much it is ("That's seventeen thousand rubles.") Now you go to the cashier and pay her the seventeen thousand rubles. With your receipt for seventeen thousand rubles in hand, you go back to the clerk, hand her the receipt and pick up your cheese.

That process is repeated for every item you want to buy—even if it's a different kind of cheese cut by the same clerk at the same counter. I have been able to buy two loaves of bread at the same time, but two different items inevitably means two different, three-tiered transactions.

Small wonder shopping wears you out! By the time you've got the ingredients for one meal, you've spent an hour in the store. Of course, that's if they will sell it to you at all.

Last Saturday, I saw green peppers in a shop, and for veggie-hungry Americans, the rule is, if it's green, grab it! The sign said the price was forty-five hundred rubles a piece (about a dollar each) so I hustled over to the cashier, got a receipt for nine thousand rubles and went back to claim the green peppers. I handed over the receipt and asked for two peppers, only to have the clerk tell me that she couldn't sell them to me until 2 o'clock. No amount of arguing could convince her that I should have those green peppers at 10:30 in the morning, and I left the shop with my canvas bag full of nine thousand rubles worth of potatoes. Those I could have.

Then there was the ice cream. One shop near my flat sells Baskin-Robbins ice cream, and about once a week I treat myself to a pint which has always been eleven thousand rubles. On the way home last week, I stopped to pick up a pint of chocolate raspberry truffle. I got a receipt for eleven thousand rubles, took it to the clerk at the Baskin-Robbins display, and opened the freezer to take out my flavor. The clerk closed the freezer door on my hand and said, "It has no price." I replied that it didn't matter since I knew the price, eleven thousand rubles. Wrong! The freezer was full of pints of Baskin-Robbins in two flavors, and the clerk was attending only that display, but I couldn't buy and she couldn't sell because someone had forgotten to mark the price. So, no chocolate raspberry truffle for me—or anyone else. For all I know, it all spoiled—for lack of a price.

As often as possible, I avoid shops altogether and buy from vendors who line the sidewalks and Metro stations all over the city. I know I can get green onions and cilantro from a woman in the *perehod* (walk-under) at the Garden Ring, and the best, and often only, tomatoes are available from a woman who sets up her table outside the post office. I buy eggs by knocking on a window in a warehouse near my flat—thirty-five hundred rubles for ten (not a dozen) and bring your own carton.

I haven't yet been able to bring myself to buy meat from a street vendor. Piles of scrawny chickens and greasy sausages on a sidewalk table leave me squeamish. But I may have to get over it and patronize my neighborhood butcher. He wields a long-handled cleaver on a chopping block set up on the back of a flat-bed truck parked near the egg window. Every day or so, he shows up with two or three slabs of beef covered by a tarp (and a swarm of flies), and the line forms quickly. But bring your own plastic bags; he doesn't wrap!

Chapter Nine

JULY HELD ALL sorts of promise. David was coming to stay for most of the summer. The pastor of our church, Wendy Taylor, and her partner, Ellen Sweetin, would be visiting, and Robyn had her visa (but no tickets yet). All these travel plans had begun to jell over the weeks since I'd come back from my Easter visit home. That blue velveteen couch, which would pull out into a double bed futon-style would get a workout.

They would all have come in June, but I had to put them off because of *profilaktika*. In late May, a notice tacked up in the foyer of my apartment building announced the annual cleaning of the water pipes throughout the city—and, by the way, don't expect any hot water for the entire month of June. Yikes!

My *hozayka* was stunned by the depth of my ignorance. It comes every June so how could I not know about it. Of course, it's absolutely necessary. Didn't I want clean water pipes? Did they not clean the water pipes in California?

She was developing a most unfavorable opinion of life in the United States.

This start-of-summer ritual is tied to the central planning ethic of the Soviet system. It wasn't just the economy and the country's defense that was built on central planning; the cities were even re-organized that way. The steam that heats the flats and the hot water that serves them is piped into each building through huge underground (and in some places above-ground) ducts from central boilers. Smaller cities just have a single plant for each; Moscow, of course, has many. And June is the time to maintain them.

Why June and not August when most of the residents of the city flee their flats for the family *dachas*—tiny plots of land in villages surrounding the cities where they manage kitchen gardens and fruit trees and camp in sheds, usually without running water or facilities of any kind? In August, *profilaktika* could be accomplished with the least amount of inconvenience to city residents. But that's when city workers leave the city, too. Who would do the work? Good question.

I loved telling friends at home about June without hot water, not because I was fazed by the practice but because of the name. *Profilaktika*, of course, brought quite another image to mind and, whenever I tried to explain the joke to Russian friends, something was always lost in translation.

Nor was the lack of hot water for a whole month much of a laughing matter. I was not into cold showers no matter how warm it was outside. I had to boil water on the stove and tend to my daily *toilette* at the kitchen sink. My mother grew up with a hand pump in the backyard of her Arkansas home so she knew this exercise well. She called it The Possibles: You wash down as far as possible, wash up as far as possible, and then you wash possible.

I got good at it too, but I couldn't ask houseguests to manage without hot water so everyone was put off until July. No matter how inconvenient, *profilaktika* made a great story.

BEFORE GUESTS AND family, another embossed invitation was hand-delivered for me at the Press Center. The United States Ambassador in Moscow was inviting me to a lawn party at the Ambassador's Residence in Moscow in celebration of America's Independence Day!

According to the English-language *Moscow Times*, more than five thousand American ex-pats were living in Moscow, a figure that made my eyes pop! Seems as if I personally would have run into a lot more of them, but I guess a city of more than ten million swallows five thousand loud and grinning Yanks in a single gulp.

But I would be one of the lucky hundred or so to snack on hot dogs and sip *shampanskoye* at Spaso House just off the Arbat on a sunny and warm July 4. A very good jazz band was playing in the garden when I arrived with my newspaper friend Paul Janensch. The Ambassador and Mrs. Pickering were pros in a reception line; they remembered my name and my story even though I hadn't seen either one since that storybook dinner in February.

As soon as I walked through to the garden, it hit me that I had missed the memo on dress. I'd worn my brass-buttoned navy blue linen suit (which would get a workout that warm Russian summer) but just about every other woman was decked out in flowery summer silks and those huge garden hats from the Ascot scene in *My Fair Lady*. The memo wouldn't have helped; nothing in my closet here—or at home—would have fit the bill. And I really hate hats!

The manicured garden was lined with super fragrant pink- and red-striped peonies. I couldn't raise peonies in California (something about the bulbs needing to freeze in the winter), but I remember banks of them lining the long walk from the street to the first house I can remember as mine. It was in the Chicago suburb of Maywood, where I lived until I was six.

Mother had a black photo album, tied with a black silk cord, with thick black pages of snapshots held in place with those lick 'em-stick 'em corners. Under each photo, my real father, the one who pretty much disappeared from my life after the divorce, had printed a caption in white ink. Many of them said, "Mick and Rookie and the peonies."

He called me "Mick," which my mother detested. She had recorded "Michelle" on my birth certificate after my father, who was an Army medic in wartime France, responded to her wire announcing my birth with: "Name her Michelle Adaire." Mother spent the rest of the years she was married to him (and many years after) calling up images of who the real Michelle Adaire might have been. He kept his silence.

(I was forced to surrender the "e" from Adaire at age five, when I was adopted by her second husband Ted—my dad.)

Those photos of a toddler me and Rook, the German shepherd who considered corralling me within that huge lawn his solemn duty, give shape to my early childhood memories, and peonies—which you can buy by the armload on any Moscow street corner in the early summer—always take me back there.

In that Spaso House garden, the bowers of feathery plate-sized peonies were set apart by carefully tended beds of the yellow and black pansies Russians call *Anyutiny glazki* or Anna's Eyes. Now that I've learned the name, I limn out the "eyes" from every pansy to find the dark doe eyes of Anna Sharogradskaya.

I recognized lots of people from a variety of NGOs that had poured into Moscow after the thaw in the Cold War. The buzz over the canapés was about recent rumors that every non-governmental organization in Russia was going to have to register as a foreign agent—the first step to limiting the wide-ranging influence they had then. A particularly shrill woman nattered on about getting all the NGOs together for some kind of pow-wow to respond to the threat.

I let all the chatter in English wash over me. After the trip to Vladikavkaz where I had to focus so hard to understand everything going on around me, this was Heaven. I could relax and soak it all in. No tension headaches today.

After Spaso House, I walked home down Stariy Arbat, past the massive and turreted Ministry of Defense and under Smolenskaya Ploschad where I stopped in the *perehod* to buy some peonies for my flat from the gold-toothed *baba* who could be counted on to be selling seasonal flowers and veggies from her *dacha* whenever she could coax something out of the ground. She was the first one selling *podsnezhniki* in March while all of Moscow was snowbound and the last one with chrysanthemums in the fall. And every bunch was the same price: *Tysyacha rubley* (a thousand rubles) was the response to *skolko?* (How much?) no matter what I was pointing to. She managed her costs by the size of the bunch: *Tysyacha* got you two peonies or one tomato but a fistful of green onions, parsley, and mixed greens (mustard, collard, occasionally lettuce).

I could count on finding her squatting on a three-legged milking stool, with neatly folded *tysyacha-ruble* notes weaved through her ample fingers, holding court over her quilt on the concrete floor of the underground passage. Lots of other vendors came and went, but she was a fixture on my way to work and back, and I counted on her.

Back home, I put the peonies in water and changed from my sensible suit to jeans and tennies for still another Fourth of July party. The American Chamber of Commerce in Moscow had erected a *papier-mâché* Statue of Liberty in a grassy field in the northwest corner of the city for an early evening picnic and fireworks show. All the young interns from RAPIC, Paul Janensch, and many of the ex-pats from other newspaper NGOs would be there. It promised to be as gritty as the ambassador's reception was posh.

Another jazz band (this one from Ukraine!) had set up a makeshift stage on a flat-bed truck next to the listing Lady Liberty, and people were jitterbugging to the mostly familiar tunes. We played softball, ate hamburgers and ice cream, sang a dreary rendition of the *Star Spangled Banner*, and saluted the flag presented by a Marine color guard.

But most of us couldn't stay away from a most unlikely Fourth of July attraction—a boneyard of mothballed Cold War-era MIG jets that dotted a couple of acres right next to the picnic site. We could climb around on the fighter planes and crawl into the cockpits. Kudzu-like vines had swallowed many of them whole, but we took snapshots of each other posing on them and waving our paper Stars and Stripes. It was another of those jarring culture clashes here that would gobsmack you when you weren't looking.

I faded before the fireworks started since it would be nearly midnight before it got dark enough, but I watched them from my balcony after I got home. It was about as close to a traditional Fourth of July as you could get half a planet from home.

THREE DAYS LATER the ever-chatty Gennady ferried me out to Sheremetyevo in his Lada to pick up Wendy and Ellen and then dropped us off near Red Square. Both of them were beyond jet-lagged, but they wanted proof they were really in Moscow. We snapped photos in front of the multi-colored and many-patterned St. Basil's Cathedral, ogled the golden domes and spires of the Kremlin churches, and peered into Lenin's Tomb. Then I herded them home for a nap (in my bed, not on the less-than-wonderful sofa bed). They had only a few hours to rest before we had to hustle off to the ballet to see *Giselle*. Unfortunately, the Bolshoi isn't open in the summer but this production at the Kremlin Palace would do. They would need toothpicks to hold their eyes open.

I was thrilled to get the chance to show off Moscow from my perspective. The next morning, a Sunday, we walked south about a mile along the river to the stunning blood red-and-white Novodevichy Convent where a Russian Orthodox service was scheduled at Smolensky Cathedral. Set apart by white stone walls from the city which pulses around it, Novodevichy has remained largely intact since the seventeenth century. I retold the stories I'd heard of the wives and sisters of the tsars (including Peter the Great's first wife) who were forced to "take the veil" at Novodevichy and be transformed into new maidens (a free translation of "novodevichy"), conveniently disappearing when they became inconvenient to the tsars.

We would spend that afternoon with the icons of the Kremlin cathedrals, and then I would show them a slice of Moscow most tourists would never see. We took the bus to Park Kultury station and dashed across the broad boulevard when a pack of snarling dogs created a traffic break. From there, we picked up a footpath that cut diagonally across a garden to a small wooden house, with a wraparound veranda enclosed with windows, tucked under a bower of weeping willows. Sheltered from the deafening bustle of the street, the setting recalled the sleepy country estates of *War and Peace* or *Anna Karenina*. I always expected to find a rumpled Tolstoy in a wicker chair napping under a tree.

This was Gurya, a family-owned Georgian restaurant that was a favorite of the Press Center twenty-somethings. It was hot (despite all the open windows), crowded, and noisy with the most pungent aromas (think freshly crushed coriander seeds and tarragon leaves). The best white beans, green beans, and beans of any shade I've ever eaten (also the cheapest) were dished out family-style with platters of lamb *shashliki* as guests pulled bottles of Georgian wine from their bags and pounded them on the table, demanding glasses. Harried waitresses (all daughters of the family, I was assured) took orders, teased, argued, slapped wandering hands, and pushed parties together to make room for more diners. Gurya was not for the meek, only the hungry.

Before we set out for Kolomenskoye the next day, I drilled the rules of Metro travel in Moscow into Wendy and Ellen. The trains we would be taking were among the most crowded in the city. Although I had no doubt that they could shove and elbow with the best of them, they needed to know the routine if we were separated: Stay in the station, at the same level, in the same spot where you got stranded; your fellow travelers will get off at the next station and come back. No need to panic; just wait.

We crossed the river at the Borodinsky Bridge (still no Gypsies), made our way to Kievskiy Vokzal Metro station and took the world's steepest escalator down, down, down. I played Mother Hen, shooing Wendy and Ellen on, and we even got seats for the first leg. We had reached our transfer station when things went to hell in a hand basket.

First, the escalator up one level was *ne rabotayet* (out of order), and we had to hike up those steep stairs to the next level and watch the train we wanted to take pull away as we huffed to get there. Not to worry; the digital clock in the station clicked the seconds off for the arrival of the next train in four minutes (and I had never known those clocks to be wrong). As we regrouped, commuters spilled down from the level above and chugged up from below. We were afloat in the human tide.

Stay together; stay together! I jostled us into position where I thought the doors would open, and we struggled to stay upright as the jam-packed train pulled in. I guessed wrong! We were half way down the landing as one throng emptied out and another pushed in. We shuffled our way to the door with me behind the other two urging them on. We would have been fine (just squished a bit) if a dozing passenger hadn't awakened to realize he had to get out fast. He spun Wendy and me in—and Ellen out—just as the doors closed.

Ellen looked stunned in our last glance at her through the window as the train gained speed. Wendy was frantic, and I was praying that Ellen would remember the mantra: Stay right there. We never moved from the door and scrambled out at the next station, ran across the platform and caught the next train back. There was Ellen, deep in concentration (perhaps it was prayer since she was a former nun) and staring at the clock as we rushed up.

We huddled on the platform as I measured their nerve for another try. They were game, and both of them showed some classy commuter moxie in getting on the next train.

KOLOMENSKOYE WITH ITS green lawns and manicured gravel paths was as serene as the train ride was chaotic. We were totally alone in the five-hundred-year-old Cathedral of the Ascension, wrapped in the silence of the cold white stone. There was no one to push us along as we stood in awe in front of the *iconostasis* and absorbed the piercing black stares from the ancient icons.

We gaped at the A-frame shape of the building, built to celebrate the birth of the *tsarevich* (young prince) who would become Ivan the Terrible. The cathedral looked nothing like other Orthodox churches with gilded bulbous domes and spires that I'd seen all over Russia.

Many of the historic wooden buildings that had survived fire after fire in Moscow had been moved to this lovely series of low hills climbing up a steep embankment from still another loop in the Moscow River. But it was sacred ground for what had once stood here as much as for what was left. Peter the Great played soldier games in the palace here as a child, and he was largely to blame for its demise when he swept the capital from Moscow to St. Petersburg.

It was well into the evening when we got back to the flat and flipped on the Powerbook. Wendy wrote a quick note to Laurie about all they'd seen, adding that it "feels so exciting to have as our guide someone who loves this city and all its history." She showed me her note, and it brought me up short. She had put her finger on something I had never admitted. I did love this place—more than I ever imagined I could.

My e-mail flash session filled my inbox:

- David had his tickets in hand and planned to stay until the end of the summer before returning to Washington, D.C., and his new job as a special education teacher in Montgomery County, Maryland.
- Robyn wanted to know if it made any difference which Moscow train station she arrived at. She had no idea there were so many in Moscow (nine!), but her itinerary listed Byelorusskiy Vokzal as her final destination. Did I know where that was? (Oh, yes. Just a couple of Metro stops from Smolenskaya. I'd be there!)
- Laurie was getting excited about the gathering at the cabin in two weeks. Twelve friends were coming, and everyone was bringing whatever food and drinks they wanted. He thought he'd bring a cabbage (!) because he'd always liked cabbage. (Married twenty-eight years and

this was the first I'd heard that he liked cabbage.) The warehouse project was still on course with just the usual bumps and twiddles. He couldn't see any reason why he couldn't come to Barcelona with me over Labor Day. He said he'd been pricing airline tickets—which was a little baffling. USIA would arrange my travel; surely he planned to fly with me!

It was still daylight when I closed the lid of the laptop and got up to make some tea for us all. No need. Wendy and Ellen were sound asleep on the world's most uncomfortable couch. I sipped my tea alone at the little kitchen table and smiled.

Cabbage? Really?

THE NEWSPAPERS IN Moscow were having a field day. Yeltsin had been rushed to the hospital with what was described then as heart arrhythmia. Since then, no one really knew who was pulling the strings of government, but the idea that there was an official puppeteer somewhere was gaining converts.

First, Associated Press in Moscow broke the story about the great photo fraud. A photo of a hale and hearty-looking Yeltsin in a polo shirt sitting by a tennis court next to a bank of phones signing legislation had been issued to quash reports that Yeltsin was much sicker than originally reported, but the picture was actually taken in April while Yeltsin was vacationing at the Black Sea. Some AP photo editor saw the fresh print from the presidential press office and scratched his chin. That photo looked awfully familiar. He went back to the archives and there it was—same shirt, same phones, same paperwork.

The irreverent (and immensely popular) *Moskovsky Komsomolets* daily in Moscow had some fun with the photos. They printed them side by side under the headline: "Can you find three things that are different?" just like the children's puzzle game that appears in Sunday comics in the States.

So who was so stupid as to risk the credibility of the presidential press office when it apparently is true that Boris Nikolayevich is indeed recovering? No one knows, but several newspapers hinted deliciously that it was the work of behind-the-scenes puppeteers who were pulling the political strings of power.

The reference to puppeteers had added significance right then since some life-size puppets in the form of Yeltsin and a couple of other political dignitaries were grabbing headlines as well. One of the most popular television shows in Moscow is a political satire called *Kukly* which means "puppets" in Russian (and for Americans of a certain age it recalls the old children's television show *Kukla, Fran and Ollie*—the puppet Kukla must have had Russian ancestry).

In one skit, lookalikes of Yeltsin and his cronies were begging alms on a Metro car crowded with Uncle Sams. Shortly after the show was broadcast on the independent station NTV, the Prosecutor General's office announced that the show's producers were being charged with "insulting and humiliating public figures."

Interestingly enough, it was the state-supported newspaper *Rossiskaya Gazeta* that spilled the beans on the prosecution and came to the defense of NTV and *Kukly*. The puppets even made an appearance at a press conference to show that it was untrue that they had thin skins. Indeed, the rubber of the puppets' bodies proved to be quite thick when it was displayed to the assembled media.

Russian *apparatchiki* (bureaucrats) have always taken themselves quite seriously, and anyone who has been able to wade through the tomes that make up the Russian press law will tell you that it works exactly opposite to the way libel laws work in the United States. American laws are built on the idea that public figures should receive the least protection since they willingly place themselves in the public arena; the greatest protection is reserved for ordinary citizens. Not so in Russia. Here the politicians protect their own hide first and foremost; ordinary folks are on their own.

But there's still another development in the *Kukly* scandal: It seems that no one knows who actually filed the claims that they had been publicly insulted and humiliated. The presidential press office denied any knowledge of such a demand.

Papers are speculating it must have been one of those behind-the-scenes political operatives or puppeteers at work again.

Newspapers here may occasionally play fast and loose with the facts, but no one will ever accuse them of being dull—not as long as there's an ego or two to pierce.

THE DRIVER GENNADY was getting rich ferrying me back and forth to the airport, but he probably would have done the deed for free when I told him that I was picking up my son. He'd peppered me non-stop with questions about my family (half believing, I suspected, that I made it all up), but now he was going to meet my son. I added that he'd be able to meet my husband in August just to pique his interest.

David, who was the image of his dad only taller (six-foot-four), arrived but his bag and guitar did not. Lufthansa promised to deliver them to my flat the next day. His bag did come but not his guitar. Three days later, when we still couldn't get anyone to tell us what was going on, the ever-resourceful Svetozarov came up with the telephone number of Lufthansa's director-general in Moscow.

Finally some answers: They had the guitar but the travel case was locked. David hadn't recorded the serial number of the guitar on his Customs Declaration (not that I'd ever recorded any serial numbers, not even for my computer) so it couldn't pass through Customs and they couldn't open it to find the number. David told them to pry the lock open if they had to. When the guitar was delivered that night, it appeared Lufthansa had used the same *instrumenty* that my "super" had used to open the deadbolt on my flat months ago. It certainly would never lock again.

Michelle and David surrounded by RAPIC interns and friends.

The RAPIC interns adopted David as soon as he arrived, and he slid seamlessly into their twenty-something world. He had a gift of mimicking the speech around him and, if you didn't listen too closely, you'd be convinced his babbling was Russian. He was a low-maintenance guest since the kids were doing all the show-and-tell. Just days after he arrived, he joined three of them on a train trip to the ancient Tatar city of Kazan, far to the east, to stay with the *babushka* one of the girls had lived with for a summer.

The *baba* had set a Tropicana juice bottle of something lethal on the table. David took a swig, and "the whole house moved. The last time I felt that was when I drank grain alcohol on that trip to Belarus." Ouch! He was still queasy when he got back.

Now that I was in the homestretch of my stay, I asked David if my decision to go to Russia had mattered to him one way or another. I guess I was still looking for vindication for my me-first choice. He had always been totally open about his emotions (really the only one in the whole family), and I knew I'd get an honest answer.

"Your going was no surprise," he said. "It was consistent with the way you lived your life. It didn't have much of an effect on me because I was in school and away from both you and Dad.

"I thought your going to Russia was cool. It separated me from my other friends and their mothers who weren't so active. I was proud of you. I'd tell people you'd written a book, and you were going to be part of a fundamental change in journalism in the new Russia."

Had Dad ever told him how he felt about it? "No, never. You're the only person Dad is honest with."

Laurie surprised me with a phone call a week before the group was going to gather at the cabin, and he wanted me to tell him that twelve people wouldn't be too many and the mix of our friends and their teen-agers would work. And then he dropped a bombshell: Had anyone e-mailed me that *The San Mateo Times* had been sold?

Whoa. That's why the publisher had refused my request for a leave of absence. A sale like this takes a lot of prep before it becomes public, and he must have known last fall that my separation from the paper wasn't going to be temporary. Even if I wouldn't admit it, I had always believed *The Times* would take me back when I got home again, that I would have a job waiting even if it wasn't the one I'd left. And now I wouldn't. I would be a fifty-year-old newspaper editor with no newspaper to edit. I was glad Laurie couldn't see how shaken I was. Even I was surprised.

THE FOLLOWING SATURDAY, the telephone rang for a second time just after three in the morning. David had called fifteen minutes earlier to say that he would spend the night at Renny's flat where he was partying since he had missed the last bus.

I had just drifted back to sleep when it rang again. I reached across the bed to pick it up, expecting to hear David's voice again, expecting to snarl at him for waking me again.

But it wasn't David.

"Micki, it's Mike," and then another voice on an extension, "and Paul."

My brain was fuzzy, but I had been thinking about those two longtime friends, Mike Venturino and Paul Anderson, who were up at our cabin with Laurie that weekend. All day my thoughts had drifted across the ten thousand miles to the good times I knew they were sharing. They were all going to call me late Saturday evening their time, Sunday morning in Moscow. But it was too early. Why were they calling so early? Why wasn't Laurie on the phone?

Mike was talking, "This is a call we hoped we'd never have to make, but we have to tell you that we lost Laurie today."

Lost? What do you mean lost? I was thinking but I didn't speak.

Then it was Paul's voice. "He was wading in the Stanislaus River, and he slipped and fell. He was just carried away over a falls. We found his body about half a mile downstream."

The word "body" bolted me awake. I couldn't scream, I couldn't speak. Nothing. I was just beginning to perceive the dimensions of the aching hole that had been carved out of my life, and I was teetering on the edge. No wracking sobs, just a choking feeling as if something was sucking air out of me—and tears, the first drops of rivers of tears to come.

Finally, I found a voice. When? Just after noon, about four hours ago.

How could that be? I was awake four hours ago, reading in bed, and my husband, the man with whom I'd shared my entire adult life, raised two wonderful children, dreamt and planned and laughed and loved, had died. How could he suffer such a violent death and I wouldn't know it, wouldn't feel it, even if we *were* separated by half a planet? Weren't we two halves of the same soul?

"Keith had these USGS maps of the Dardanelles area so we decided to go hiking up there," Mike explained. "We took two cars and drove about twenty-five miles on up Highway 108 toward Sonora Pass. We turned off at the bridges over the Clark Fork and Middle Fork of the Stanislaus. It's been really hot, and Laurie kept saying he couldn't wait to get his feet in the water.

"The rest of us were looking at the maps and talking about the area, but Laurie took off his shoes and waded into the water."

Paul picked up the story. "The rivers are really full because of all the rain and snow last winter, and he must have slipped or tripped. But as soon as he fell, he was gone in an instant. Some saw his bright blue shirt shoot past, and then he was over the falls. No one saw him again until we found the body."

"He must have been unconscious almost immediately," Mike added. "The boulders are huge, and the river drops so fast. I'm sure he never knew what happened."

Another long silence.

That's what we did every summer. We'd wade in the rivers and skip rocks, and Laurie would lose his glasses. The streams of the Sierra are paved with Laurie's glasses. I bet that's what he was thinking when he fell: I'd better hold onto my glasses.

I felt myself smiling at the thought. Strange, how could I smile?

"Is David with you?"

"No, he's spending the night at Renny and Julie's." My voice was almost a moan. Oh, God, we've got to get home.

Mike had already made two sets of reservations for us—one on the 7 a.m. Lufthansa flight, Moscow to Frankfurt to San Francisco, and another on the noon Delta flight, Moscow to New York to San Francisco.

"I don't see how we can make the Lufthansa flight, but I'll call you and tell you how we're coming. I have to call David now—and Robyn. I hope she's not alone."

I sat on the bed for several minutes, shaking and hugging my knees. Finally my need to have David with me overcame my horror at having to tell him. I reached for the telephone and then realized I couldn't remember Renny's number, a number I called routinely nearly every day. I had to turn on the lamp to find it. The light made my head throb, and I dialed as fast as I could make my fingers work.

The music and laughter were loud when Renny answered. I tried to control my voice when I asked for David, but I clearly hadn't succeeded.

"It's your mom," Renny said, handing the phone to David. "She's crying."

It took me a few seconds to make David understand, and then he let out a wrenching scream that shut out the party sounds in the background. When he spoke, there was silence in the background. "I'm coming, I'm coming right now."

David tried to dash out of the apartment, presumably intending to run the two miles or more to my flat, but Renny and another friend Megan held him until they could leave too. They flagged down a car on the Garden Ring to bring him home.

The next call would be harder. Robyn was so far away, and I wouldn't be able to hold her and cry with her. I thought of waiting until I was back so I could tell her in person, but what if she heard it from someone else? I had to tell her. I dialed her apartment in the Mission District of San Francisco, and she answered.

Was she alone? Yes, her boyfriend was at work. Could he come home? Maybe, what's wrong?

"Oh, Robyn, I hate to have to tell you this from so far away," I stopped and took a breath, "but . . . Daddy died today."

No, no, no. Her anguish was piercing, and my attempts at comfort were useless. We cried together on the phone. It would be more than thirty hours before I could hold her.

David still wasn't back, and my loneliness was suffocating. I walked out onto the small balcony above the embankment and watched the first rays of sun dapple the water of the Moscow River. This tame and sullied river had given me comfort every day of my seven months in Moscow; now another river, the wild and angry Stanislaus half a world away, had snatched my husband away.

There, on the wrought-iron balcony in the thin light of a new Moscow morning, the sobs heaved up within me, and I found my own moaning wail.

I heard David thumping up the stairs. He was beyond distraught, sobbing and writhing as I held him. He finally collapsed on my bed as I tried to console him. Renny and Meghan stood over us. How could they help?

Renny called Gennady and arranged a ride to the airport. Meghan pulled my suitcase out of the closet and began packing the things I could think of. She made tea and asked direct questions when I was making no sense. I got the cash from the freezer and gave Renny enough money to pay my rent and asked him to call my *hozayka* to explain what had happened.

Should I tell her you'll be coming back? I don't know. I can't think right now. Just pay her for August, and I'll let you know when I get home.

And then it was quiet.

Renny and Meghan left after I insisted we'd be okay. David was asleep on the bed, exhausted and spent. I couldn't allow myself to measure the hole in my life, not now. Now I had to keep moving, keep on keeping on. I had to get us home where our support system was, where Robyn was.

Gennady was in the foyer when we got out of the lift about eight that morning, and he took our bags without a word. The Delta reservation counter was pure chaos, but we had no boarding passes, only the reservations Mike had made. David, still crying but softly now, waited with the bags while I joined the scrum. Once I got the attention of one of the harried agents and he located our reservation, I asked if I could upgrade our tickets to Business Class since we were returning because of a "bereavement."

What do you mean?

My husband died yesterday, and we need to get home.

Lady, Delta didn't have anything to do with that. The plane's full. Got it?

The flight attendants took one look at us and led us to two seats alone by the window in a spot where relief pilots rested on long trans-Atlantic flights. It had a curtain that could be Velcro-ed into place if we wanted it. I sank into my seat, totally empty. For the next nine hours, nothing would be required of either of us.

David's voice was gravelly. "The last time we talked we argued about that library book. That was the last thing we had to say to each other." I squeezed his hand and recalled that Laurie's and my last words had been that telephone conversation when he told me I had no job to come back to. Now I had no husband either.

We had a couple of hours' layover in New York, and this was going to be hard. I had to make calls to family. When I'd called Mike to tell him what plane we'd be on, he told me that the story of Laurie's death was on the news so I couldn't take the chance that they would hear from someone else.

I found a pay phone where I could sit down and stacked up all the quarters I'd been able to gather. I dialed Laurie's sister Jeannie in Kansas City. I didn't want to have to tell his widowed mother without someone with her. No answer.

My throat was parched, and David was running back and forth getting me Diet Cokes and finding more change. I was able to get my folks in Minnesota, but still no answer at Jeannie's. Finally, I called Laurie's best friend Bill Frederick. His wife Sally answered. Bill wasn't home but she would get a hold of him, and they would go to Jeannie's house to wait for her. It was several hours later, while we were in the air again, when Bill, Sally, and Jeannie went together to tell his mom.

Once we were headed to San Francisco, I pulled out my Powerbook, set it on the tray table in front of me and clicked it on. I opened a new document and started typing.

What are you doing?

I'm writing your Dad's obituary.

How can you do that!

David, this is what I do. I'm a writer so I write. And who better to write this than me?

Who, indeed?

Laurence Roy Carter
March 25, 1944-July 29, 1995

Memorial services will be Sunday for Laurence Roy Carter, 51, of San Mateo, who drowned Saturday in Tuolumne County.

A local service will be at 8 p.m. at the Congregational Church of Belmont, 751 Alameda de las Pulgas. Another service will held at 2 p.m. at John Knox Village in Lee's Summit, Missouri, for his family and friends from the Kansas City area.

Carter, a native of Salina, Kansas, had been married for twenty-eight years to former Times Managing Editor Michelle Carter. A graduate of the University of Missouri at Columbia, he had lived in San Mateo County since 1967.

He had been a systems analyst for Del Monte Corporation in San Francisco for twenty-five years. At the time of his death, he was consulting on a warehouse automation project for Del Monte in Stockton.

Active in the Congregational Church of Belmont since 1975, he was moderator this year and had sung in the choir for many years. He was chairman of the church's major fundraiser, the Chocolate Fest, last year.

He also was the financial officer for the Children of Chernobyl Project of Northern California and had traveled to the Chernobyl region of the former Soviet Union in 1992 to deliver chemotherapy drugs and medical supplies to hospitals in Belarus, which are treating children affected by the 1986 explosion at the Chernobyl nuclear reactor.

Carter was a musician who played the organ and piano and sometimes served as a substitute organist at the church.

His many hobbies included astronomy and studying the night sky from the Carter family cabin in Long Barn near Sonora. He flew to Hawaii in 1991 to see the solar eclipse. He coached AYSO soccer from 1981 to 1983 and served as president of the San Mateo-Foster City Babe Ruth League from 1987 to 1989.

Besides his wife, he is survived by his daughter, Robyn of San Francisco; his son, David of San Mateo; his mother, Gene Carter of Lee's Summit; and his sister, Jeannie McGuire of Overland Park, Kansas.

Memorial donations may be made to the Music Fund of the church or the Children of Chernobyl Project, 751 Alameda de las Pulgas, Belmont.

Chapter Ten

I WAS SUCKED dry as David and I dragged ourselves off the plane at SFO after eighteen hours of exhausting travel and the gut-wrenching phone calls in New York, but the sight of more than twenty friends, crowding around with love and concern gave me a huge boost. Ryan Anderson, Paul's son who had lost his own mother, my friend Bette, almost exactly a year before, grabbed David in a bear hug, and Wendy and Ellen swallowed me up. Thirty hours after the phone call in Moscow, we were home.

But Robyn wasn't there.

I thought someone would pick her up since she didn't have a car; everyone else thought she would meet us there. I was frantic to have her with us so one car headed into the city to get her while the rest brought David and me to the house in San Mateo where friends had been answering the phone all day. News of Laurie's death had moved on the Associated Press wire, probably because his was the fourth drowning at the same spot this summer, and had been reported on local radio and TV. The word was out.

Once I had Robyn close by, we pushed through the curtain of fog to make some initial plans: The memorial service would be the following Sunday evening to give my folks, my brother, and Laurie's mom and sister time to get there. Paul and Mike would take the three of us up to the cabin the next day so we could see Clark Fork for ourselves, arrange for the cremation and sign papers at the Sheriff's Office.

When they first called me, I had begged them to tell the rescue team that Laurie was a registered organ donor and to do everything they could to harvest anything, including his corneas. All his adult life Laurie had been a regular donor at the Blood Center of the Pacific. He was Type O Negative, the universal donor. When an emergency call went out, he would dash out to give blood on his lunch break. When California began registering organ donors and putting the information on drivers' licenses, Laurie and I were at the head of the line.

I had not the slightest doubt that he would have wanted to donate his organs, but those four hours Laurie's body remained in the water, caught on a fallen tree, while the rescuers stretched tackle across the rapids and winched a rescuer over to retrieve him, had allowed his organs to degrade. How he would have hated that!

I don't remember anything else from that day except getting into bed. I'd slept there alone many times. Last fall, when Laurie started the Del Monte warehouse project, he often stayed in Stockton overnight. Four years before he'd gone to Hawaii alone for a few days to watch the solar eclipse. And, of course, I'd been alone for seven months in Moscow. But when I laid my head on the pillow, I could smell him in the bedclothes, and it ripped the scab away.

Sobbing into the pillow, I suddenly knew I was replacing his smell with my own and I would never be able to get his back. I pulled the pillowcase off and pawed through his shirts in the closet, burying my face in them one by one, searching for his scent. They just smelled of Tide. The dirty clothes hamper was empty, but there on the desk someone had placed his duffle bag that he'd brought to the cabin directly from Stockton. It held two rumpled oxford-cloth shirts and a pullover, and I could smell him in them. I tore the protective covering off a suit just back from the cleaners and wrapped the dirty shirts and pillowcase in the plastic. This is what I had left of him. I was frantic to save it.

Eventually I mined the entire house and the cars, tucking away snippets of his distinctive all-caps printing and cassettes with his comments on music he recorded for the cabin. ("That's all, folks! That's all there is" at the end of one tape.) It would be nearly a year before I could replace his message on the answering machine. I only did it then because I overheard someone saying it was macabre.

ON MONDAY, ROBYN, David, and I stood on the ribbon of gravel along the edge of the angry, roiling Clark Fork of the Stanislaus River, swollen past flood stage and hiding the seventy-five-foot cataract where it spilled into a granite-walled ravine and surged on to meet the Stanislaus on its way to irrigate the Central Valley of California.

Over the years, we'd picnicked beside and waded into most of the forks of the Stanislaus and the Tuolumne, but we'd never been to this spectacularly beautiful spot. Even if we had, it looked nothing like it must have looked earlier or how it would look when we returned year after year. This winter had seen record-setting snowfall in the Sierra, and it was still melting at mid-summer, turning ambling streams into churning furies. On the previous Friday, at this very spot, it had snatched a six-year-old girl from her parents and pulled her over those falls. A hand-painted sign stood as a memorial to the child whose body was never found. On Saturday, it had taken Laurie.

Paul and Mike, both still shaken, replayed the tragedy for us, and it made horrible, mind-bending sense. Laurie had been driving our Plymouth Voyager van with four others inside. Everyone else could see the waterfall as they crossed the bridge over Clark Fork, but Laurie had his eyes on the uneven pavement ahead. The day was blistering hot, and he said he wanted to get his feet in the water. The others laughed him off; the water was too cold and too fast. Geologist Keith Howard was spreading out some maps; others were unloading the cars. No one noticed as Laurie headed down to the river, pulling off his shoes.

Mike turned from the group and saw Laurie in the water up to his knees, facing away from him, with his shoes and socks sitting on the exposed granite rock that served as a beach. He wanted to warn him to get out of the water, but he was afraid he'd startle him. He ran down to the river in time to see Laurie lose his footing and slip.

Laurie had always worn old tennis shoes in the water because he had to protect his right foot. He'd cut off the four smaller toes on that foot in an electric lawn mower accident the day before he was to graduate from high school. In closing the wound, the surgeons had wrapped skin from the top of his foot over his missing toes to cover the ball. The bottom of that foot was so tender he never ever went barefoot outside—except this time.

Ellen McCarty had been lathering up with sunscreen when she started toward the river and saw Laurie sitting in the water looking shocked just as the bright turquoise of his T-shirt zipped away in the current.

A Northwestern University journalism student, Ellen gave me an amazing gift. She had taken the time to write an account of everything that had happened that weekend. Thanks to her journal, I could see for the first time how this ordinary summer day with old friends had pitched into hell in a matter of seconds.

Laurie had been in a great mood all morning, teasing Ellen about her Yoga poses and threatening to fry baloney for breakfast. Mid-morning, he, Paul, and Mike decided to cut down a small cedar that was crowding a couple of other trees next to the cabin. After some serious hacking with a big-toothed handsaw and lots of kibitzing, they posed for a snapshot next to their conquest. It was the last photo of Laurie ever taken.

Paul, Laurie and Mike with the fallen cedar.

Ten of them packed a picnic and headed east toward the Dardanelles, a unique rock formation on Highway 108, past Pinecrest Lake, in a two-car caravan. It's about a forty-minute drive from the cabin to the Clark Fork turnoff where Keith's USGS maps showed some hiking trailheads. Keith parked up the road under a tree, but Laurie, who seemed to be fixated on cooling off in the river, left the van closer to the bridge.

Running up from the river, Ellen and Mike screamed for help while Paul dashed across the road and followed the river from the boulders above the south side. Others scrambled down through the manzanita bushes on the north side, but they could all see him floating face-down in the river, snagged on a fallen tree, about fifty yards from the falls in a spot where no one could reach him.

Mike and Keith's wife Linda jumped in her car to find an emergency roadside telephone. With Mike behind the wheel, they sped out to the highway and raced east to Kennedy Meadows where Mike knew they could find a ranger station. Not long after they made the call, a red and white CalFire helicopter hovered over the river and directed the Tuolumne County Sheriff's swift-water rescue team to the site. No need. They already knew the spot; they'd been there the day before.

Ellen, her parents, and sister stayed at the river another three hours while the rescue team strung tackle across the river to secure Laurie's body and then lift it out of the water. Laurie's leather key fob was wet and cold when one of the rescuers pulled it out of his jeans pocket it and handed it to Warren, Ellen's dad. Now they could drive the van back to the cabin.

THAT MONDAY MORNING we had two more stops to make. At Heuton's Memorial Chapel in Sonora, the mortician already knew that Laurie would be cremated and that he wouldn't be embalmed. I expected to be pressured to "upgrade" our choice. I'd written a series of articles about the gouging practices of the funeral industry, and I stiffened my shoulders and lifted my chin to show my resolve. But no need, the mortician just recorded the details. I signed some papers, wrote a check for nine hundred dollars, and rose to leave when he stopped me. Would I like to view the body?

One more gut punch, and I crumpled.

I didn't want to see him. I wanted to carry with me the image of him waving goodbye at the airport in April. I didn't want to see him beaten down, as physically battered as he had been emotionally for most of the time I'd been gone. I shook my head.

"I want to see him!" David was adamant, so he and I followed the mortician into the next room. It was a mistake to see him bruised and scraped raw after the pummeling he'd taken from the granite boulders of the cascade. Back in the car, I had to sit very still to focus on not throwing up.

The sheriff had Laurie's wallet, coin purse (one of those rubberized ovals that gaped open when you squeezed it), and his belt for me to take home. I had to initial the notation on the form: *No jewelry recovered.* Laurie had a beautiful 18-karat gold band in his top dresser drawer—the one I put on his finger at our wedding—but he never wore it. He didn't wear a watch either although he often kept a wrist-watch in his pants pocket. He just didn't like to have them on. It had never bothered me, but I had the sense that the sheriff didn't approve.

As I was leaving, he added that I was really lucky that they'd recovered Laurie's body. "Most the time, we don't, like that little girl. But he was a good-sized man and he got snagged. It's a whole lot easier this way, believe me."

I'd take his word for it.

The chief of the swift-water rescue team came into the office as I gathered up the papers, and he shook my hand.

That was a tough one Saturday, he said. That cataract at Clark Fork falls into a rock-walled chasm that's no more than three feet wide through the narrows. The water was moving at close to five thousand cubic feet per second. He didn't suffer any. It was all over in an instant.

For some reason, his words wrapped me in a thick blanket of comfort.

I'd taken a number of photos of the river so I could put together a narrative for the memorial service that Laurie's friends were planning at John Knox Village near Kansas City on Sunday, the same day as the service here. Laurie's mother chose to attend that service rather than make the trip to California although Laurie's sister Jeannie and her son would come.

I wrote them about the visit to Clark Fork. "It helped immensely to see the river and feel its power. I had a strong sense that Nature had taken back one of its own and, in selecting one, chose the best . . . I had twenty-eight years of a great partnership with a man who understood me and could support me without ego. I can only hope that our marriage provided him with all that he needed.

"At one place in the Gospels, Jesus describes his disciple Nathaniel as 'the one without guile.' That was Laurie."

AT HOME, FRIENDS had been doing all they could to help—laundry, cleaning, answering the phone and the doorbell, and finding room in the refrigerator for all the food that was arriving. The dining room table was left for things only I could deal with, including a detailed log of messages and a small mountain of mail. Someone had sorted out the ads and third-class mailers for recycling, but the rest (dating from the Monday before, the last time Laurie was home) had to be opened.

Someone brought me tea as I dug in. I set the cards aside for a quieter time and started on the bills. Two envelopes from Bank of America caught my eye.

Congratulations! BofA was returning to Laurie and me a copy of the mortgage for our San Mateo house with PAID stamped across it. The second letter was identical—but this mortgage was on the cabin. I sank into a chair to try to take this in: Fourteen days before he died, Laurie had paid off the mortgages on the house and the cabin!

In the bedroom, I pulled out the binder where he recorded mortgage payments and other big transactions and ran my finger down the list of entries marked July 15. He must have devoted the day to putting all our finances in order. He closed out several CDs, paid every outstanding bill, wrote two checks to Bank of America (where he'd drawn a smiley face next to "free and clear") and then opened a new five-year CD with the interest rate (7.25 percent) and maturity date noted.

He'd left me a map for my financial future although he couldn't have known how critical it would be so soon.

Laurie and I had taken out new life insurance policies before I left for Russia. It seemed to be a smart idea since I would be assuming some new risk for the next year. It had been comforting, over the past few days, knowing that I would have that insurance settlement as a financial cushion to see me through next few months without a job (*The Times* was no longer an option), without health insurance (my coverage ended when Laurie died and I had a pre-existing condition, a stroke when I was thirty-eight, that made it just about impossible to get a new policy), and without my kids (Robyn would be joining David on the East Coast, looking for a job in New York City). Life was piling on.

When I called the insurance company to file a claim on Laurie's policy, they delivered another hit. In California, I was told, insurance companies had up to ten years to pay up if the insured died in the first year of the policy. Somehow we'd missed that.

I REMEMBER VERY little else from that week. Friends handled housing arrangements for my brother Bob, Laurie's sister Jeannie and her son Brian, and my mom and dad. Mother had wanted to come immediately when I called but I put her off for later in the week. We'd never had the kind of relationship that I so envied in other friends and their mothers. Her presence wouldn't comfort me; it would just add to the stress.

I had never been able to be the daughter she expected me to be, and at some point I quit trying. As a kid, I must have been a handful with a "smart mouth" that she answered with a slap across the face that could draw blood. If that didn't do the trick, a wire flyswatter lashing on the back of my legs usually would. But I was so "bullheaded" (her word), I refused to cry. I'm sure it would have ended sooner if I had.

Things came to a head one afternoon when I was a junior in high school. I came home to find both my mom and dad waiting for me in the dining room of our suburban Chicago house where we moved (from California) during my sophomore year. On the table were two packets from colleges that I had written away for.

My dad pointed at them. "What are these for?"

I wasn't expecting this.

"I'm a junior. It's time for me to start picking a school."

"You think you're going to college?" Mom picked up the packets and hurled them across the table at me. "Then you just go to college!"

Message received. Once again I didn't know my place, I was trying to be better than everyone else, better than she was. She was a bright, strong-willed woman who'd been shackled by circumstances (the Depression, the war, a failed marriage, and me). She'd be damned before she'd give me what she never had.

I got it. No more college catalogues came to the house. I had them sent to a friend's house, and we pored over them together while I figured out how I could get there on my own. I worked fifteen-to-twenty hours a week at Jewel Foods, a Chicago-area grocery chain, all through high school, and they offered their part-timers the chance to earn college scholarships. The winners got several thousand dollars for college expenses and—most important of all—a well-paying job every summer during college.

I won a scholarship, and the photo of my mom and dad grinning (with what . . . pride?) as I accepted the award at the banquet still stings. The first thing I did after arriving at the University of Missouri in Columbia (alone, on the train) was to have my seventeen-year-old self declared an emancipated minor. Now the university would deal with me alone.

Once Laurie and I were married and half a continent away, feuding with my mom lost most of its appeal. We lived our lives, and she tsk-tsked from a distance. She didn't have a clue why I would leave my husband at home and spend a year in Russia, but she said she wasn't surprised, considering how little I cared for what people would think (one of my major character flaws). And I admit I didn't waste any energy trying to explain.

I was relieved that friends from the church offered to house my folks for their stay.

THE MEMORIAL SERVICE was lovely, with eulogies from Paul and Laurie's Kansas City childhood friend Gary Hearn and music from both Caz Chorale, led by Mike, and the Sanctuary Choir. Just a couple of weeks before he died, Laurie had played John Rutter's "The Lord is My Light and My Salvation" as special music at church so the choir reprised it in the service. It was glorious.

As the memorial ended, we all heard Laurie saying, "That's all, folks! That's all there is," on the cassette we retrieved from the cabin.

So many friends filled the church that the sanctuary doors were opened onto the veranda where more folding chairs were set up. I felt truly blessed, but I was blown away when I turned to greet a group I didn't recognize. Turns out, they were Laurie's Del Monte co-workers (forklift drivers and warehouse office personnel) who had caravanned from Stockton to say good-bye to him, someone they said they'd come to respect and appreciate as a friend. Having them there was huge for me.

Then, at the end of the reception line, a woman took my hand. "You don't know me, but I know all about you." She handed me a card with at least fifteen signatures.

"We're the CalTrain bridge players!" For nearly twenty years, Laurie had commuted to the city and back on CalTrain. Morning and evening, he always looked for one of the cars with facing benches and a table that pulled up from the wall so that a rotating group could play bridge en route. In the card were handwritten vignettes that told me Laurie stories I'd never heard before.

How he played matchmaker for a pair of bridge regulars who couldn't seem to see that they were meant to be together. (He was best man at the wedding!) How he always had a box of popcorn he bought at the station and how he almost always spilled it at some point during the game.

What a lovely gift!

I opened another gift that night when I gave up trying to sleep and flipped open my laptop to slog through an avalanche of long-neglected e-mail. Among the condolences was a note from Oleg and Elena: Their eagerly anticipated second child, a daughter named Anastasia, had been born in Moscow—on Saturday, July 29, the very day Laurie had died.

THE NEXT MORNING, my brother Bob, Jeannie, and her son Brian joined David, Robyn, and me and a number of other friends (including Paul and Mike) on a trip back up the mountain. We stopped in Sonora to pick up Laurie's ashes. I listened to the mortician spell out the California law about properly distributing what he called "cremains" (which made me cringe!) and then accepted the plastic two-gallon container (a whole lot heavier than I expected).

The river-rock memorial for Laurie.

We wanted to scatter his ashes in places that Laurie loved. Most of them were at or near the cabin. We started at Clark Fork where we arranged rocks to spell out Laurie's name in a clearing next to the river, very close to the spot where the rescue team recovered his body. A piece of the tackle was still hanging from a Sugar Pine near the water. We took turns spreading ashes in the clearing.

Pinecrest Lake, a favorite summertime family spot, was still so full of snow run-off that there wasn't much beach. We chose a not-so-crowded spot where a couple of Ponderosa pines stood with their roots submerged at the edge of the lake to scatter more. Dodge Ridge, where we'd skied as a family from the time the kids could walk, was closed for the summer, but no one stopped us from climbing up the wide swale known as the Ridge Run to leave something of Laurie on his favorite ski trail.

We stopped at the North Fork of the Tuolumne, where it comes within two miles of the cabin, and then at the outcropping of the logging road where you can see Yosemite Valley's Half Dome to the south. We walked down to the creek in the national forest that we could still hear rushing at the cabin, and we hiked up to the clearing of scarred lava rock east of Long Barn where the kids had been convinced a meteor had imploded.

At each spot, we'd just remember and leave something of him. On the way back to the cabin, someone said, Laurie would have loved this.

At home, I had a special place to leave some ashes. In the backyard, a level rectangle on an otherwise uphill lot, I'd planted a Eureka lemon tree that had never produced a single lemon. Laurie hated it because he had to mow the lawn around this obstacle. I spread a film of ash around the roots of that Charlie Brown lemon tree—and the next year, for the first time, I had lemons!

Jeannie and Brian took some ashes back to Laurie's mom in Kansas City where boyhood and college friends had gathered around her for a memorial. Jeannie said she would find the chance to spread some on the lawn of their childhood house on Charlotte Street in Kansas City as well.

AND THEN IT was quiet—empty, clock-ticking quiet.

Everyone was gone: Robyn back to the city; David off to Washington, D.C. to start his special ed job; and friends back to their own lives. I sat in that echoing silence, drinking tea and trying to imagine how I would restart my life. The quiet was deafening.

I had to cut through the fog and make some decisions.

Would I go back to Russia? Everyone would understand if I didn't, but I had so much I'd left undone. The book on newspaper design for Russian editors was the most obvious, but maybe I could finish that from home.

Could I really put the burden of packing up my apartment on friends at the Press Center? They would do it in an instant, but that would be so much to ask of anyone, let alone kids who never understood why I needed to create my own nest in Moscow, why I needed a real home there, not just a place to crash.

Would I have to give back a big chunk of my grant if I didn't stay for the time I agreed to? I was surprised how much I was worrying about money. Rough calculations showed I could live, without a job, for several months, maybe even a year or two, especially now that I didn't have mortgage payments. But I would be cutting into savings, drawing down IRAs, things Laurie would never have done. I was just fifty, a good fifteen years from retirement when all our long-planned investments would kick in.

Laurie had always been so confident and in control about our finances. Even though I understood everything (he'd left such a clear road map!), I'd never been so totally at sea about it all. It wasn't as though I was clueless. I knew the answers were inside me somewhere but I couldn't access them. The links were broken. I didn't feel like me anymore.

I just wanted to talk to him. I wasn't ready to be alone.

I had spread out Laurie's wallet and everything in it to dry on the faux wood surface of our desk/work table in the bedroom, and I kept returning to re-arrange things so air could get into the folds of the wallet. The sheriff had urged me to throw it out, ("Wet leather starts to smell and stiffen pretty fast.") but I couldn't. Leather cleaner had (mostly) restored my boots in Moscow; I was sure it could save the wallet.

I'd used flat-edged tweezers to peel the photos and cards from the pockets. There was almost no cash, a chronic condition for Laurie, but I was desperately hoping to salvage the black-and-white print of my engagement photo that had appeared in the *Kansas City Star* twenty-nine years ago that month. It had been in the window of every wallet he ever owned.

It had required surgical precision to separate the photo from his first California organ-and-tissue donation card. The state had since adopted the "pink dot" on the driver's license, but Laurie had hung on to his original. How he would have hated to know he would die without the chance to donate his organs.

For some reason, he still had his draft card from 1962, the year he turned eighteen, graduated from high school and cut off his toes in the lawn mower accident. His classification was 1-Y, given to those who were limited in their ability to serve but not disabled. (The fact that most gay men got the same designation made for plenty of Sigma Chi house ribbing.) In the early seventies, Laurie got a new card classifying him 4-F (unfit to serve) but that one was nowhere to be found.

He'd kept his Eagle Scout card even though I knew he considered himself something of a fraud as an Eagle Scout. To rise to that level of scouting, he had to complete a major project. His was a working telescope, but he confessed that his dad did most of the work on it. He loved the friends he made in scouting, some of them lifelong, but he had no interest in climbing to the pinnacle of the organization. That telescope, however, made its way to the cabin and served deck duty on many a starry night with Laurie giving guided star tours.

Once they dried, I pressed the paper items in encyclopedia volumes in between sheets of waxed paper. The wallet, dry and restored with leather cleaner, went to David at Christmas that year.

I WANDERED FROM room to room, sitting perfectly still on the deck, listening for . . . I don't know what. My senses were hyper-alert. A cool breeze was a rasp scraping at my bare skin, and any unexpected sound jolted me upright. I'd turned into a terrible passenger when someone else was driving. I shot my hands out in front of me when the car braked and dodged and cringed when cars got too close. I'd never done that before.

If this was grief, would it matter where I grieved? This house that had been our home for twenty-five years didn't feel like home anymore. I got no comfort from it. I'd once interviewed the Swiss psychiatrist Elisabeth Kubler-Ross about the stages of grief for a newspaper article. I knew I had to will myself through this shadow and come out the other end, but did it matter if I was in this house or in the flat by the Moscow River?

If I was going to be alone, at least there I was used to it.

But I knew I was kidding myself if I thought of my Great Adventure as any test of independence. All the time I was in Russia, I had a well-oiled support system spinning the dials and pushing the buttons at home. Laurie had been managing our finances in both dollars and rubles for the past seven months. I just sent him the raw data in my Quicken uploads, and he kept me on pace and on budget. I'd miscalculated my Synthroid usage and was running out. No problem. He got it refilled and shipped it to me via DHL. Homesick? I knew I could make one very expensive phone call and hear his voice any time I really needed to.

I may have been living a solitary life in Moscow but I was never alone.

I finally pushed through the sludge to see if I could get enough information to form a decision. I called Valerie at USIA to see where I stood on my grant. To keep the money, I would have to go back to Russia, but she would take the finished design book in trade for the month of August (spent at home) and trim a few weeks off the end of the stay. I could come home in November.

But the grant was also providing more than income. It was my only source of health insurance as well. An afternoon on the phone confirmed that very little had changed since Laurie and I had tried to find a company that would cover me. The stroke I'd suffered at age thirty-eight created a nasty pre-existing condition.

The stroke was quite a public event. David was playing in a Little League championship game, and Laurie and I jumped up to cheer at the end of the game. I felt a blinding stab behind my left ear and crumpled to the ground. I lost consciousness for a few seconds but, when I woke up and saw everyone huddled over me, I just wanted to get away.

Laurie helped me to the car since I couldn't seem to walk by myself. I was sleepy and wanted to go home and nap. He was having none of it. We were at the ER in a few minutes. The rest of that day is mostly a blur except for all the diagnostics that required fluids and dyes inconveniently kept on ice on a Sunday afternoon. I was so cold I couldn't stop shaking despite the need for me to remain "perfectly still."

My right side was failing. All day it took more and more concentration to wiggle my toes—until it was dark and I couldn't move them at all. I sank into black quicksand that night but by morning, I'd started climbing out. I could twitch my toes a little. By the time I left the hospital two weeks later, I'd regained almost complete use of my right arm and leg. I could type (thank God!) but my grip was mostly gone.

Laurie had a fix for that. For months, he would stand on a tennis court and toss balls to me. At first I couldn't even keep the racquet in my hand, but by the time the winter rain forced us inside, I could return the balls over the net. I loved tennis and hated physical therapy so we combined the two. I still have trouble lifting full pitchers or cooking pots from the stove, but I'd always considered my recovery complete (and I'm still playing tennis).

While I was in the hospital, a Stanford University researcher interviewed me as part of a study linking strokes in relatively young women to those early estrogen-packed birth control pills. I'd taken them as a teen to regulate my non-stop periods. They worked wonders but apparently left a debt to be called in twenty years later.

Health insurance hadn't been a problem as long as Laurie and I were working. It came with the job, with or without a pre-existing condition, but no longer.

I'm not sure which consideration shifted the balance—or maybe it was the path of least resistance—but I decided to go back.

Valerie wanted me to talk to someone from USAID in New York, someone who might have a job to offer, so could we meet there on my way back to Moscow? Absolutely. Barcelona was no longer on the itinerary. Laurie and I had put so much into planning our getaway there that I couldn't face it by myself.

I sent my regrets.

Letters From Russia
Life is what happens when you're making other plans

SAN MATEO — I was supposed to be coming home this week for some R&R before the last stretch in my appointment in Russia. And, finally, my husband would be going back with me. His plans to come to Moscow in March and May and July had all been scuttled by delays in his work project, but this time he had his plane ticket.

But, of course, he won't be coming now.

Our plans and the lives of our children and myself were changed forever with a phone call to my Moscow apartment in the middle of night on July 29. Laurie had drowned in the Stanislaus River on a weekend outing with friends.

My son David was with me in Moscow, and we held each other up over the next eighteen hours of air travel that brought us back to San Mateo. We were met by many of the same friends who had sent me away with much to-do last January.

I have lots of photos from that January departure and, looking at them now with a different eye, I can see some apprehension in Laurie's face. He had been absolutely adamant that I should accept this appointment as the USIA Journalist-in-Residence in Moscow when the offer first came last September. But in the excitement of launching my Great Adventure, I never calculated the depth of the sacrifice he was making.

We were both "nesters," quite comfortable to allow home and family to limit our career choices. Shortly after our daughter Robyn was born, we agreed that we would both make our careers here in the Bay Area and that neither of us would accept job changes that would move us away. Each of us had passed up at least one significant career opportunity to stay put, and I don't think either of us ever regretted it.

But this appointment in Russia would only be temporary. He understood the fascination that the former Soviet Union held for me since I first traveled there eight years ago.

He too had been caught up in the magic of the place when he joined me on a humanitarian delegation in 1992. We were in Belarus to deliver food and medical supplies in a particularly dark period after the breakup of the USSR. He went off alone in a truck with a Polish driver to make a food delivery in the small city of Stolin, about six hours' journey from Brest, where we were staying. His adventure, including his introduction to the Russian tradition of vodka toasts, were the stuff of legend when we returned.

"Everywhere I went, they told me I was the second American ever to come to Stolin. The first was our friend Mike who'd been there two days before. I felt like Buzz Aldrin, the second man on the moon."

So it was decided that I would go. To do that, of course, I would have to leave the security of *The Times* where I had worked for twenty-seven years. For Laurie, who had been out of work for seven months just a year before, that may have been an even greater jolt. But he never winced, never offered a second thought. "You've been moving toward this for the last eight years. It's the right thing to do, and it's only ten months. I'll be here when you get back."

On our twenty-eighth anniversary on January 28, we were apart for the first time.

I had not even the slightest premonition that twenty-eight years would be all we would have. We had planned to go to Maui for our twenty-ninth since Hawaii in January seemed to be the exact antithesis of a winter in Moscow. A flier for a condominium resort in Wailea was on his dresser when I came home last month.

In these awful last days, friends and acquaintances have told me how proud Laurie was of me and my work. He passed out copies of my e-mails and sent tearsheets of my columns to family and friends across the country. As lonely as I know he was, he sent me strength when I was the most homesick. He kept reminding me of the importance of what I was doing and noting that I was one-quarter, one-third, one-half of the way through the separation.

And so I'm going back, and my daughter Robyn will be with me, perhaps for the whole two months that are left. I will finish what Laurie and I started. The excitement of the Great Adventure in Moscow is over, and this new adventure of life alone is simply scary. But the work's not done, and he's still sending me strength.

I'll write when I can.

Chapter 11

THREE SMALL VASES of late summer asters and mums were lined up in front of the door to my flat when I got back. My *hozayka* (landlady) must have let my neighbors know when I'd return, but I was grateful for the silent welcome.

The heat of the summer was gone, and the thin, slanting rays of the autumn sun felt good in the chill of the flat. The sun would sink behind the Kiev railroad station by five, and the days would get shorter at a much faster pace than at home. The trees on the *naberezhnaya* (embankment) below my windows were already shedding their fall brilliance. Through the thinning leaves I could see those huge ravens, called *vorony*, darting among the branches with the sun flitting over the wet iridescent sheen of their feathers. Those were the biggest, blackest (almost purple really) birds I've ever seen— the reason, I'm told, that Moscow has no squirrels!

I was beyond exhausted, and the muddled brain I'd experienced in the month at home was no better, perhaps worse, since I now had to slog through the mental muck to find my Russian. Conversations that had been quick and easy before were a struggle all over again.

Gennady had been mercifully quiet on the ride from the airport, except to tell me that he was sorry that he never got to meet my husband—and that he was emigrating to Israel at the end of the year!

On one of our earlier trips out to Sheremetyevo, he had told me that he and his wife wanted to leave Russia and join a cousin in the States. He had gone so far as to spend an entire day in the visa queue at the U.S. Embassy in Moscow as it crawled along the block and switched back across several streets, creating an ever-present traffic jam. But all he got when he made it inside was an application and an appointment to return it once he'd filled it out. After several interviews, he would then be rewarded with a chance to take part in a one-in-a-million lottery for a visa.

But Israel offered a direct route out of Russia. And from there, he said, who knows? I eyed the Orthodox cross dangling from his rearview mirror. Wasn't emigration to Israel limited to Jews? He just shrugged. He could be a Jew.

More than a million Russian citizens took the same path in the years after the fall of the USSR, and the question—Who is a Jew?—still stirs passions in Israel today.

Because Jews were so widely persecuted in the former Soviet Union, Israel threw open its door for them. On my first trip in 1988, I'd joined another member of the delegation to carry documents to a *refusenik* couple, Alexey and Sveta Petrov, in Leningrad (St. Petersburg today), who wanted nothing more than to emigrate to Israel, but it was official Soviet policy to "refuse" any Jew's request for an exit visa. Because the Petrovs were so brash as to ask for one, they were under constant watch.

The instructions for our meeting with them, arranged by a *refusenik* support group in California, read like a John le Carre novel: Take this Metro to this station, get out and take the next train back two stations, walk out and catch this bus, get off and retrace the bus route on foot to this street. Someone (Smiley?) would meet us there and escort us to their flat.

We weren't very good at it. A greasy-haired man in a shiny maroon jogging suit, carrying a matching gym bag, stuck half a block behind us all the way back to our hotel. I saw him at least three more times in the hotel lobby while I was there. He stared straight at me, unflinching when I returned his look. He never said a word to me, and he never changed his suit. Surely someone was going to stop us at Passport Control at the airport on our way home and utter those gut-punching words: Step aside, please.

It never happened. The maroon-suit man hung around, I supposed, just so we would know that they knew.

Alexey and Sveta, fired from their university professorships, were barely getting by when we talked, but they were desperate to get their teenaged son out even if they couldn't escape. The papers we brought were intended to help with that cause. We talked with them for most of an afternoon, and I later wrote stories in *The Times* about their plight. The whole family was finally able to leave about a year later when Gorbachev's policies of *glasnost* and *perestroika* (openness and transparency) reached full flower, and *refuseniks* were no longer refused.

After the end of the Cold War, other Russian friends, stymied by America's visa morass, had opted to emigrate to Canada. The Canadians (with one-ninth of the population of the U.S. spread over twice as many square miles) had a great visa scheme: Produce proof that you had fifteen thousand dollars in cash or in a bank account, and the gates swung open.

However he managed it, Gennady would be on his way at year's end, but he swore he would still be in Moscow in November for my last trip to the airport. After all, he was my driver! He pulled his Lada into the driveway behind my building and offered, for the first time ever, to carry my bags up to my flat. No need, I assured him. I was fine.

I was so fine, in fact, that I stared blankly at the keypad at the door, burrowing into my brain to pull up the entry code (409, the kitchen grease-buster!) until the family on the floor above me came out to walk Dawg, their Great Dane, and I nodded and slipped in after them.

I set down my bags, and it was the first time in my flat all over again. Leaning against the inside of the door, I could see into all three rooms, but what I was missing most had never been there at all. I slid down the cushioned Naugahyde to the floor. This is what my Great Adventure had come to: Me and my aching emptiness, sitting on the floor of my apartment, half a planet from home, with everything behind me and nothing ahead. No sobs, no screams, nothing.

I DON'T REMEMBER crawling into bed, but it was noon the next day when I woke up to a chilly drizzle. Sleep had helped. I wouldn't say I was energized but I knew I needed to act as if I was. (Fake it 'til you make it!) I needed to start moving and see if things would click into place.

The flat was spotless, but dishes were put away in the wrong cupboards and clothes in the wrong drawers. My *hozayka* had been in to lend a hand while I was away. Those orange sateen drapes once again were hanging in the living room hiding my view of the river through those tall, double casement windows. Those ugly drapes poked something inside me. I climbed up on a chair, unhooked them and let that high, flat light flood into the room. I folded them away for another two months.

She'd even taped the door to block the wind off the river, but it wasn't nearly cold enough for that. Off came the tape perhaps a little too eagerly; a patch of paint pulled away from the woodwork. Now I'd have to see if I could hunt up some eggshell enamel to match for a repair.

I was hungry for the first time in a long time. She'd left some eggs and cheese in the little German refrigerator and fresh *lavash*, the Georgian bread I bought by knocking on a shuttered window in the next street over. I ate too much too quickly and felt a little sick, but even that was something—better than nothing.

I HAD TWO weeks before Robyn was coming with a fellow traveler who'd been a roommate in the Santa Cruz bungalow that lost its chimney during the epic Loma Prieta earthquake of October 1989. Santa Cruz was just about the epicenter of the 7.3 quake, and the university took a direct hit.

Laurie and I were anxious because we couldn't get through to Robyn. Reports out of Santa Cruz described lots of damage to some of the university buildings which had glass panels stretching three stories up. We thought she would have been working the school switchboard, one of her part-time jobs, just after 5 p.m. when the temblor struck but, with no telephone service, we couldn't reach her.

I was at *The Times*, of course. Most of the editorial staff had made it back, and we were working through the night, wading through broken glass and spilled photo chemicals without power or phones, to put out a special edition once the computers and the press came back online.

About nine thirty that evening, John Brooke, the pastor of our church, showed up in the newsroom after a slow crawl across town. Turn on NPR, he said. We'd been listening to local news on a transistor radio, so I turned the dial to National Public Radio and heard her voice! Robyn was interviewing students and detailing the damage. She worked for the campus radio station (KZSC) and happened to be there when the quake hit. She grabbed a microphone and was on the air in minutes. Seems we were in the same business after all!

John had been at Candlestick Park for the ill-fated Giants-A's World Series game with David that day so he could assure me that David would be home as soon as the car he was in made the slog through the snarled traffic.

I was hugging John with relief just as Laurie showed up with Coleman lanterns and sandwiches. The only damage at our house, he reported, was a jagged crack in the dining room ceiling, some spilled canned goods and a garage door that had slipped off its track. Oh, and both our cats (who spent most days hissing at each other) were snuggled up together in the clothes dryer and quite happy to stay there.

Robyn's off-campus bungalow was barely habitable since the chimney in the yard wasn't the only casualty. She and her roommates, including the one she was traveling with this fall, camped on the lawn for some time, along with a good portion of the rest of Santa Cruz, as aftershocks kept everyone on edge.

In a little more than two weeks, her train would arrive at Byelorusskiy Voksal. I'd be normal by then.

AT THE PRESS Center, Svet was certain all I needed was to get back to work. I wanted to finish the booklet, *The Contemporary Guide to Newspaper Design,* so Tanya Patina could start translating it. I'd laid most of it out on PageMaker in early July but I'd need the Cyrillic text to complete the project and create the file for publishing. To my great relief, a fax waiting in my mailbox confirmed that USIA would accept the book and time spent in-country as fulfillment of my Professional-in-Residence contract.

While I had been in New York on my way back to Moscow, my USIA handler Valerie suggested that I might want to write a couple more manuals for Russian editors, including one on newsroom management. She thought she could swing another grant for them, and I could do most of the work at home. (Sounded like a paying job.)

This also would mean that I could keep Tanya working as well. I'd been trying to ease her into a bigger presence at the office after she traveled with me to Novosibirsk and two other Siberian cities last spring. A gifted interpreter (in five or six languages!), she got a kick out of adding "newspaper-ese" to her resume. I hoped she'd be well-situated to stay on there after I went home.

Besides, on the road with Tanya was rather like traveling with Anna Sharogradskaya—I didn't have to fuss over trains, airplanes, hotels, or documents. I didn't have to think—beyond my dog-and-pony show, which Tanya probably could have given herself! She mothered me, even though I was twenty years older. Under normal circumstances, I would have pushed back, but not now. I don't quite remember where we were, but one time I told her I needed a bathroom *now*! In seconds, she'd found one and (no doubt) pulled the current occupant out so I could get in.

On a trip to the southern city of Astrakhan, she'd been a blessing. I'd been invited to spend a hands-on week at the major newspaper in this grimy industrial city on the lower Volga where it spills into the Caspian Sea, the largest enclosed body of water on Earth. (It's also the source of much of Russia's caviar, which I'd come to love. At home it was a delicacy; in Moscow it was everywhere and fairly cheap!)

The oily air in Astrakhan was so polluted (think Beijing on a bad day) my contact lenses felt like sandpaper, but everyone at the newspaper was upbeat—eager to learn and to show off their corner of Russia. It didn't take me long to pick up that the paper, and especially the editor, was under siege from the local autocrats who ran the city, and this visiting *Amerikanka* might just be in the line of fire. What started as a snafu at the hotel (sorry, no room!) ballooned into a tug of war over my *dokumentii*.

I'd surrendered my passport to the hotel clerk when I arrived (the usual practice in Russia) just before she announced that we'd have to find another hotel. I knew the editor had made reservations so we got him on the phone and he came over. After much haggling, rooms—different digs for *inostrantsi* (foreigners) and nationals—happened to open up.

Despite the niggling, my room looked much like every other provincial hotel room I'd been in, complete with what I'd come to call the "coffin" bed—a narrow twin with a low wood railing on three (and sometimes four) sides intended, I was sure, to discourage noisy love-making. The ballroom-sized bathroom had the usual showerhead at the end of a hose and no shower curtain. I'd never got the hang of washing my hair without spraying water all over the room. The hose was quite manageable hanging limp on its hook, but as soon as you turned the water on, you had to wrestle it for control.

On my way out the next morning, I asked for my passport as I did at every other hotel. Sorry, not yet.

Why? Shrug.

Tanya picked up on something not quite right long before I did. Could we see it?

It's not here. It's at the mayor's office.

Why?

They came and got it. If you want it, you'll have to go there. Stop asking me for it.

Uh-oh. Now I was an *inostranka* in a provincial Russian city without my passport and visa—as my mother would say, "Up shit creek without a paddle."

Back in the newspaper office, we huddled over strategy. The editor was convinced that he (a *persona non grata* in Astrakhan) and even Tanya would make things worse if they went with me to the mayor's office so I would go alone.

All morning I sat in that office, which could have been any bureaucratic department anywhere in Russia. I'd seen the very same blond wood paneling and the same blond wood *shkaf* (cupboard) with the smudged glass doors hiding the same dusty tchotchkes in administrative offices all over Eastern Europe as well as Russia. Finally, the clerk I'd been staring at all day told me that my passport wasn't there any more. It was at the police station.

Same routine at the police station in what could have been the same office. (Russia must have kept factories running 24/7 producing nothing but blond wood office furniture.) But the chief of police wasn't quite as busy as the mayor. Just about dinner time, the door opened and his eminence (burly with dark Stalinesque features) appeared—holding my gorgeous blue American passport!

The deal was simple: I'd get the passport at the airport on my way out of town that evening. He added a string of qualifiers but I didn't understand them. The editor and I traded our "so sorrys," and Tanya and I got out of Dodge.

ASTRAKHAN CONFIRMED MY suspicions: The farther you got from Moscow and St. Petersburg the less you find you actually know about Russia. I'd been to Vladivostok on the Pacific a year before, and Cyrillic characters and the *khruschovky*, those sterile apartment blocks, were about all I could recognize as Russian. It could easily have been in another country.

Now I was about to stretch that idea even further. Svet was proposing a trip to Chelyabinsk, a grimy industrial city in southern Russia that hosted the Soviet Union's top nuclear weapons manufacturing complex, Mayak. It was known as the cancer capital of the world.

The tragedy of Chelyabinsk occurred not in one dramatic reactor explosion like Chernobyl, but rather in a tortured assault played out from the late 1940s through the 1960s. It gave this region on the eastern slope of the Urals, at the edge of the Asiatic plain, the highest concentration of cancer cases of any region in the world, and no one had a clue at the time. Stalin's cult of secrecy had drawn a steel curtain around the issue so complete that even the people who were living there were ignorant—until the explosion at Mayak in 1957.

The Mayak nuclear complex dumped its waste into Karachay Lake and the Techa River, which fairly regularly turned black from the deadly effluent. Residents of Chelyabinsk, on the banks of the Techa, stayed out of the water when it was black, but otherwise continued to use it as they always had—for fishing, swimming, boating, and drinking.

Then in 1957, a temporary waste disposal site exploded sending a radioactive plume into prevailing winds that carried it across Siberia. In 1967, a prolonged drought caused Karachay's shoreline to recede by a third leaving a parched lakebed powdered with radioactivity. The following summer a windstorm whipped the dust off the lakebed and spewed it across very nearly the same territory as ten years earlier.

So, all in all, a nasty place, but Svet kept prodding me to go. I would be the guest of a superb editor, who had led his newspaper, the *Chelyabinskiy Rabochiy* (Chelyabinsk Worker), in a campaign to reveal the secrets of Mayak and the ecological crisis that still gripped the region. Svet even enlisted Tanya to go with me. He wanted me to get back on the horse. I had two weeks before Robyn would come, and I'd reached a stopping place on the book. Now or never, I supposed.

At least we wouldn't have to fly Aeroflot. We had tickets on TransAero, a new private Russian-British joint venture that would have made any western carrier proud. TransAero charged almost twice as much as Aeroflot but you didn't hear anyone squawking. They flew Boeing 737s and, once inside, you could be on United or Delta. The worn carpet and seats testified to the age of the plane, but everything worked just fine.

I'd flown TransAero to Novosibirsk last spring, and the flight was so pleasant I'd neglected to prepare myself for coming down—physically and mentally. Russian pilots have a habit of descending far faster on a much steeper slope than western pilots and, on the flight home from Novosibirsk, we came down so fast, I had to dash to the bathroom as my stomach lurched up into my throat. I was still there when we touched down. I'm no fearful flier, but that was a first.

As soon as we landed, we climbed down the stairs to the one antique bus waiting to take an entire 737-full of passengers and their hand luggage to the terminal. The ground attendant helped push us all on, and I got my first look at the snowy splendor of the Siberian taiga with my face smashed against the filthy back window of the bus.

The terminal, with its mish-mash of modern technology and fifties furnishings, reminded me of another arrival at a provincial airport in the Urals. I had been blown away to see a portable conveyor belt roll up to the plane's baggage compartment. I watched my bag float along unbattered into the terminal where, I was sure, it would slide onto another conveyor to circle around and around until I picked it up.

Uh, no. My bag glided into the building only to be dumped about eight feet onto a pile of other bags on the floor of the terminal. An empty baggage carousel wheezed and whined in the center of the room, but the bags all fell well short of the mark. I had to paw through the mound of luggage to rescue my suitcase, which has limped as it rolled forever after.

But my stay in Chelyabinsk was an awakening. Once just another Gray Lady of the Soviet era, *The Rabochiy* now championed the growing ecology movement in Russia. Over dinner with one of the leaders of a local conservation group, I learned that a recent Freedom of Information filing in the U.S. had revealed that the CIA had known all about Mayak for more than thirty years—but had kept quiet.

During the fifties, the U.S. was promoting nuclear energy as the safe and simple answer to America's escalating energy needs with very nearly the same slogan that the Soviets were offering their citizens, "A peaceful atom in every home." American scientists had no better grasp of how to dispose of nuclear waste than their Soviet counterparts. So somewhere in official Washington some gray heads nodded knowingly—and the conspiracy of silence about the nuclear disaster at Chelyabinsk a half a world away was joined.

I'm not sure that Chelyabinsk gave me a jump-start, but it did remind me why I had chosen to come to Russia in the first place, why I still believed in the project, why I needed to finish what I'd begun in a different life, in January.

IT ALSO HELPED fill the time until Robyn came. Before, it was Laurie's e-mails and our Sunday phone calls that had anchored my days. I would collect snippets and stories and jot them in my journal so I had lots of color to share with him. I was still making notes but whom was I going to tell? The joy had escaped like air from a punctured balloon. Everything left was flat and ragged.

Everyone wanted to help. My neighbors brought pots of soup, and my *hozayka* left symphony tickets. The twenty-somethings at the Press Office tried to include me (the age of their mothers) in all their doings. I mostly begged off, but a new Australian friend, Alan Dodge, wouldn't let me off the hook.

The director of the Art Gallery of Western Australia in Perth, Alan was in Moscow to lay the groundwork for what would become an exhibition of Russian art from the turn of the twentieth century for his museum in Perth. One of his contacts in Moscow was the wife of the librarian at the Press Center, so the RAPIC library became his unofficial office in Moscow. Gay, with a partner in Perth, Alan was the perfect companion for recently widowed and noticeably brittle me. If he went to the ballet, I went to the ballet. If he went out to dinner with five or six others, I did too. For my last two months in Moscow, Alan was my life preserver. He kept me afloat. I would not slip below the surface on his watch.

WALKING DOWN THE Byeloruskiy Vokzal platform marked "Berlin," I recognized Robyn's military parka and combat boots before I could see her face. My beautiful counter-culture daughter and her traveling partner from her Santa Cruz days (known forever after as Weird Wayne) strolled toward me. I knew she wouldn't want me acting the way I was feeling so I satisfied myself with just a brief hug and shifted gears from thrilled mama to host in a foreign land.

Robyn had studied Russian for a semester at City College of San Francisco so she could decode the Cyrillic and toss off enough phrases to allow her to wander freely through the city. Her take on Moscow: "Mercedes and Prada sandwiched between slabs of Soviet drab, the layers—old and new, alike—stained in something Dostoyevskian and timeless." (Surely she got her writing chops from me!)

She spent a lot of her time hanging out in the *perehody* (the pedestrian tunnels under the wide, traffic-snarled boulevards), "listening to the kids there playing Sex Pistols covers with acoustic guitars strung over their shoulders with rope." She especially loved the *rynok*, the sprawling open-air market, sometimes covered with a roof of sorts, sometimes not, where you could buy fresh fish by the kilo and cheesy sateen drapes by the yard. Some were permanent and some seasonal, but mine was just past Kievskiy Vokzal, across the river via the Borodinsky Bridge. (I didn't bother warning her about the Gypsy hordes. For Robyn they would have been an attraction.)

The location next to the train station was no coincidence. Vendors would haul their wares into town in pre-dawn darkness, hawk their goods all day and then head home after the commuter rush in the evening. Most were farmers or fishermen or craftspeople from surrounding villages, but many were *biznesmen* from the Caucasus or the 'Stans who brought in cheap appliances and cheaper clothes. The noise (bickering, yelling, cursing, and laughing) vied with the smells (from rancid to rich) and occasional blood splatter from the slaughterhouse set to send the squeamish packing. But don't forget your perhaps bag! Perhaps you would find something terrific!

The remnants of Soviet Gigantism (Moscow's Echo Radio once joked that the USSR bragged about producing the biggest microchips in the world!) and wall-sized Cold War propaganda posters around the city fueled Robyn's penchant for the *avant-garde*. Years later, she gave me a framed set of Russian magazine ads from the fifties, complete with propagandist images and slogans.

I'd been planning for months to take her to the third-floor apartment near *Patriarshiye Prudy* (Patriarch's Ponds) where a scene from Mikhail Bulgakov's brilliant satire *The Master and Margarita* was set. The concrete walls of the stairwell were splashed with bold phantasmagorical murals depicting some of the action of the novel, including the appearance of Satan as a ball of fire. It would be the premier stop on a tour of Moscow's quirky sights—even if Fodor wouldn't give it a mention.

One of the RAPIC interns took me the first time after a concert at nearby Tchaikovskiy Zal (Hall). We'd stuck our heads into two or three dingy apartment doorways until we found the right one. But when I went back a few days before Robyn arrived to retrace my steps, the entire apartment block was scaffolded and under *remont*. I nearly cried. Even the tiny Café Margarita nearby—where you could get directions to the flat if you asked—was boarded up (although it was open again before I left).

Robyn reveled in Moscow's mashup of old and new, treasure and tacky, bauble and blah, but she couldn't blend into the street crowd as she would have liked. Other girls her age wore mini-skirts and fishnets, but she claimed she was too much a weather wimp to brave Moscow's October chill bare-legged. In parka and military boots, she just drew puzzled stares.

Robyn hadn't a clue why I had come back. Surely anyone would accept the death of a spouse as a reasonable excuse for chucking the whole experiment. Later, though, she wrote me, "Now I get how throwing yourself into work is a way to cope. And if only time heals, or least mutes the pain, then why not drown it in the extremes of mid-nineties Moscow? There was something especially poetic about the fact that the obligation was journalistic—exposing/announcing/revealing—at a time when your impulse was probably to turtle."

I held it together fairly well while she was there. I remember only once retreating to my bedroom and burying my face in one of those big square European pillows. Tears were never far from the surface, and something about Robyn and Wayne sniping at each other seemed to set me off.

OLEG AND ELENA'S new baby girl Nastya had arrived the day Laurie died, and Robyn and I wanted to see her and big brother Gleb so we set off on the *electrichka* out to Tscherbinka. I knew how crowded the trains got on weekends so we planned a mid-week trip but, if anything, the Tscherbinka train was packed even more tightly than before. For nearly half an hour, Robyn and I were pressed against opposite walls near the door of one car, holding hands threaded between people so we wouldn't get separated. Neither of us could face the same return trip so I flagged a car and negotiated a ride to the Moscow end of the Metro line when we headed home.

I was incredibly relieved when Oleg and Elena moved to a flat in Moscow a couple of years later, and I no longer had to endure the *electrichka* ride to Tscherbinka. However, I'd be hard-pressed to top my first trip when I'd had Oleg as a guide. The train ride was uneventful, but when we got to Tscherbinka, a freight train was parked between the station and the bus stop. The freight didn't present much of a problem for most of the commuters; they just stepped up between two of the cars and climbed over the coupling.

I started walking along the freight to go around when Oleg said that would take too long and we'd miss the bus. We should climb over.

I'm sure my mouth dropped open. I couldn't imagine climbing over a freight train under any circumstances at home, but when in Moscow . . . I handed Oleg my bag, slung my purse over my shoulder, hitched my long skirt into my belt and stepped into the gap between the cars. I got a good foothold where my leather boots wouldn't slip, pulled myself up onto the coupling, and climbed to the middle.

I was feeling quite proud of myself until the train lurched forward.

I later told friends I had a very clear image of this blonde *Amerikanka* in a red knit hat clinging to the back of a freight car as it rattled along to Leningrad and screaming bloody murder. Oleg shouted for me to jump while the train was just inching ahead. Other commuters who were planning to follow me over the coupling had all backed away. It was clear I couldn't jump clear of the tracks from my current perch; I would have to jump down and then out.

So I jumped—down between the cars and then fell backward out from the tracks just as the train moved on. As Oleg pulled me up from the snow, my light blue coat bore the evidence of my close call: A wide swath of greasy dirt from the freight car was smeared across my chest and the back of both sleeves since I had pulled my arms back to clear the train.

We were late when we got to the apartment, but we had quite a story for Elena.

AFTER TEN DAYS or so, Robyn was ready to move on. She was meeting her boyfriend in New York City where they planned to find jobs and an apartment. She had some cheap stand-by air fare from Luxembourg to Rekjavik to Washington, D.C.—something only Robyn and some other shoe-string travelers would ever consider. We set off across town to one of the few spots where *inostrantsy* (foreigners) could purchase train tickets, and I wended our way through the web of train schedules and the usual snarky bureaucracy to see how close to Luxembourg a Russian train could carry her. The answer: Frankfurt—and she'd leave from Byelorusskiy Vokzal in two days.

The process of getting her train ticket underscored one of the reasons why it wasn't a great idea for her stay any longer. As much as I craved having her near, I could see she was chafing against the need to have her mom, the Russian speaker, run interference for her. She'd stepped out from under my wing even before she went off to college. She didn't relish being cooped up under it again as a young woman.

I helped her settle in on the train. She would share a compartment with a young Russian couple and their pre-schooler son who took to Robyn immediately. Even before I left, he was calling her *tyotya* (auntie) and climbing the ladder to her top bunk. It was a much better situation than sending her off for a day and a half with a car full of soccer players or *biznesmen*. I told the young woman that Robyn was my daughter, that she was an *uchitelnitsa* (teacher) and that she was heading back to the United States. She assured me she'd take care of her. I'd later kick myself for not giving her my telephone number and getting hers, but their little traveling party seemed absolutely perfect for sending Robyn on her way.

Over the next thirty-six hours, the image of that young family comforted me. I knew I wouldn't hear from her until she got to Frankfurt, but she had money and plenty of food to eat and share and, best of all, she was incredibly resourceful.

But when I didn't hear from her by bedtime the second day, I was antsy. I told myself she couldn't find a phone or figure out how to use the German phones, that she didn't want to wake me, that I'd hear first thing in the morning. Forty-eight hours and still nothing. I needed help but I couldn't leave the flat. I might miss her call.

Frantic, I called Svet and asked him to find out if the train had mechanical problems or anything that might explain the delay. He got the whole Press Center office involved, but the answers held no clues. The train had arrived in Frankfurt only a few minutes behind schedule and without incident. The Frankfurt police had no report involving a young woman of Robyn's description.

Maybe she just forgot, everyone kept saying. You know how kids can be. They forget. She'll call when she remembers, you'll see. I knew she wouldn't forget and, if I didn't hear from her soon, I'd go to Frankfurt myself. I couldn't do anything from my flat but I couldn't leave either. She might call.

I sat on my bed within arm's reach of that toy phone, willing it to ring, shivering, breathing in gulps. I had never been a worrier before. Our family had always mused that Laurie was the designated worrier. But I guess I'd picked up the mantle and, forever more, I would worry for both of us.

I prayed too, even though I don't believe in a God who intervenes to sort things out. The God I was praying to would understand that I needed Robyn to be safe so I could go on going on. It wasn't a prayer for intervention; I asked for mercy—the most selfish of prayers.

Who might she call if she couldn't call me?

David? Neither she nor I had his new phone number yet.

Her boyfriend? He was traveling across country from San Francisco to New York expecting to meet her.

The only reason she wouldn't call is because she couldn't. If I didn't hear from her by the end of day tomorrow, I'd have to go. I'd get one of the interns to stay in my flat in case she called but I'd go to Frankfurt myself. Our friend Mike Venturino, a United captain, could get to Frankfurt for free. Maybe he could meet me there.

Now it was four and a half days since I'd put her on the train. I couldn't wait any longer. I'd made an airline reservation on Lufthansa to Frankfurt on the 7 a.m. flight and called Gennady to take me to the airport. I was chipping ice from the ice tray to free up some cash when the phone rang. I grabbed it and heard a man's voice with a thick German accent.

"I'm a doctor at (garbled) hospital in Frankfurt," he said. I couldn't make a sound.

Robyn had been his patient, and she asked him to call me to tell me she got sick on the train but she's all right now. He had just taken (or maybe sent) her to catch a train to Luxembourg to resume her trip. She would call me from the airport.

The boulder rolled off my chest.

It would be some time before I got all the details in an e-mail from Robyn: "On the train, I came down with the worse kind of stomach bug I have ever experienced: vomiting, diarrhea (in that awful little train toilet), fever and hallucination. The walls would painfully pulse and wrinkle. Each color and texture was less a visual image and more a palpable ache or stab. The mom tried giving me pills. I had no idea what they were and figured I wouldn't be able to keep them down even if I took them.

"In Frankfurt, I found a cab and got myself to a hospital. Eventually a doctor spotted me lying on a bench somewhere. I was stabilized and allowed to stay for a couple days to recover. I was treated like a strange specimen. Being from San Francisco made me exotic, riding a train from Moscow to Frankfurt made me reckless, and being an American meant I didn't have health insurance so the hospital computers didn't know what to do with me."

She had tried calling me from the hospital over and over, but the call wouldn't go through.

She says she doesn't remember much else about that trip home, except for an announcement on Icelandic Airlines about O.J. Simpson's not guilty verdict. I'd been surprised to discover, while I was home, that I'd lost out on an entire chunk of American pop culture by missing the media circus around the Simpson trial. The BBC reported the facts of the trial from time to time, but the merry-go-round of supporting characters escaped me completely. Someone had made a Kato Kaelin joke while I was home, and I'd just stood there blank-faced.

Letters From Russia
Wild West is still alive in Russian Far East

VLADIVOSTOK — If you ever wondered what happened to the Wild West, I can assure that it's alive and well in the Russian Far East. Cities like Vladivostok on the Pacific and Khabarovsk across the Amur River from China are wide open, just as rowdy and unconventional as the American frontier was a century ago.

A cowboy mentality rules although the people in white hats are known as "reformers" or "democrats," the ones in the black hats as "mafia," and it's Let's-Make-a-Deal time on every street corner. Americans and Japanese with businesslike briefcases of dollars and Russians (or Kazakhs or Uzbeks or Mongols) with their dollars in fist-size wads vie for the spot on top.

All this flourishes in a region that two years ago was closed to the West altogether, in cities that look much like every other city in this massive country that covers one-eighth of our planet's land mass.

I was part of a group of seven American newspaper people in the country to meet with independent newspaper editors and publishers in the fall before I arrived in Moscow as the new PIR. We were there to offer advice and help in establishing a viable free press in Russia.

We got there via Alaska Airlines' in-on-Tuesday, out-on-Thursday route that unloads fishermen headed for Pacific fleet trawlers and timber men from Anchorage in Magadan in Siberia, Khabarovsk and Vladivostok and brings them home for furloughs when they've had all they can take of the murderous cold and bland food.

Alaska is America's cowboy airline. A flight crew from Long Beach (of all places) flies in from Anchorage with a mechanic/technician, interpreter and weight-distribution planner on board since you never know what to expect in the way of support services on the ground. The captain and co-pilots themselves man the de-icers and the twig brooms used to clear the windshields.

And they're ready for anything, even getting frozen to the tarmac in the minus 18 degree cold of Magadan, some 500 miles north of Vladivostok. They have no answer for the bumpy, concrete runways (sort of) cleared of snow and ice by a truck pulling a jet engine pointed up, but they wrestle their MD-80s into the air between chit-chat to calm the passengers and on-air arguments with air-traffic controllers who don't understand their urgency to GET OUT OF THERE.

In Vladivostok, Americans find a city that, from a distance, looks much like San Francisco. It climbs steeply out of four jeweled bays in a series of green hills, and the sun sets not over the Pacific but behind North Korea. But the likeness disappears up close where drab Soviet-era apartment buildings and shuttered doorways line the streets. As in most Russian cities, any notion of landscaping is a capitalist idea whose time hasn't yet come.

By most accounts, the only truly functioning administrative agency in Vladivostok (and the Primorye region) is the mafia whose leadership, by some accounts, includes the governor whom President Boris Yeltsin has seen fit to keep in place. A CNN report broadcast while we were there described how the reformist mayor had been dragged from his office by outlaw goons. His son was convicted of a trumped-up crime and sentenced to seven years in prison.

However, the local newspaper people didn't bat an eye over all this; it's business as usual in Vladivostok.

After a reasonably comfortable overnight train ride, we found ourselves in Khabarovsk, which is about the same size as its more celebrated neighbor (about 600,000 residents) but with a more European look to its broad, tree-lined avenues.

However, we were assured that the political situation in Khabarovsk was much more tightly screwed in place than in Vladivostok. Perhaps. The administrators are mostly post-Soviets who have changed their uniforms but not their stripes, and the criminal element is every bit as present. Casinos (with operators who choose their clothes from old reruns of *The Untouchables*) are easier to get into than restaurants and appear to operate with a wink and a nod from the authorities.

Newspapers in the Russian Far East fit the Wild West mode as well. There are plenty of them that appear and disappear in rapid succession, much like businesses of any other ilk. The lines of direction from political authorities still exist, but are so murky and fuzzed over, it's nearly impossible to follow the paper (or money) trail.

Editors aren't particularly interested in hearing about an industry ethic that would prevent them from accepting money for running puff pieces about businesses disguised as news. And when you're never quite sure who your boss is, it's hard to play a watchdog role. Nonetheless, they like the idea of newspapers as the Fourth Estate; it's just that they need to make a buck first to stay alive—a notion we can appreciate in the States as well.

The streets were filled with used right-hand-drive Hondas, Toyotas and Nissans imported from Japan. (When my son was in San Mateo's Sister City Toyonaka to play baseball a few years back, he said there were no old cars in Japan. Now we know where they go.)

There's a sense of well-being that seems to come with the cowboy mentality which was welcome after the monotonous doom and gloom of other Russian cities. For all its shortcomings, the Russian Far East is alive.

Chapter Twelve

EVERYONE SAID RUSSIA wouldn't be able to let me go. I thought they were just being kind, but they were right on so many levels.

I was sure I was ready. The manual on newspaper design was finished, and I'd delivered the final document to the publisher. Before the end of the year, boxes of the booklets would be shipped to regional press centers all across Russia. I was leaving behind something tangible, some physical proof of time, energy, and passion spent in fulfilling that promise I'd signed onto just one year ago.

Back then, I was bracing for a Great Adventure, preparing to test myself in a country ten thousand miles from home. I was full of bravado, stretching the limits of my tether—until it slipped its mooring. I'd been floating free for three months now, and I'd learned I'm no good at it. I needed to find firm footing again, solid ground where I could inch my way toward something new and untested. What awaited me at home would be far more foreign than anything I'd faced in Russia.

As I was taping those packing boxes that had been folded flat against the wall in the hall closet back into shipping containers, my USIA handler Valerie called. The call itself was unusual. Valerie always sent detailed e-mails, but I suspected the call was to gauge my strength as much as anything. She had no news about possible grants for future newspaper manuals (sigh), but she asked if I felt up to taking on a quick project outside the brief of my contract. I told her that Svet's conviction—that I just needed to get back on the horse—had been mostly true. Chelyabinsk had provided, if not a boost, at least a swell to see me through the last few weeks of my stay. She'd piqued my curiosity. What project? Where?

The press center in Riga, Latvia wanted me to talk about newspaper design and offer critiques at a three-day conference of regional editors in just a few days. The agreement Valerie and I had was limited to the eleven time zones of Russia (eleven, rather than the usual nine, since I'd been to Kaliningrad, a little pie-shaped slice of Russia separated from the rest of this vast country by the Baltic States).

Valerie had shared a pre-publication copy of my design manual with the USIA chiefs who handle the other states of the former Soviet Union, and the group in Riga jumped in with the invitation. They'd pick up the tab for my travel (night trains there and back), and I'd be their guest at a posh hotel on the Baltic Sea. What's not to like?

She added that she'd checked my visa to make sure I still had two exits—one for the Riga trip and that last one for home. My unlimited entry-and-exit visa had expired while I was home. My new one was limited, and I needed to pay careful attention.

Newspaper critiques in Riga.

The conference in Riga buoyed me. I felt a real sense of collegiality among the editors, rather than the distrust and fear of spilling corporate secrets, which had been so common on many other trips. For much of the time, editors crowded around me as I scanned newspapers spread out in front of me, pulling out a gem here or suggesting a fix there. I did a lot of cross-pollinating, and my briefcase bulged with Russian examples of good design. (This works for them; it may work for you.) I'd come to believe that those observations were the real value of my time in Russia. It wasn't so much what I brought from home, but what I could share of the best I'd seen while I was there.

RIGA ITSELF WAS lovely, unusually warm and sunny, the perfect showcase for the spectacle of brilliant fall colors. The beach on the Baltic Sea is covered in marble-sized pebbles, and I crouched over the stones, searching for a chunk of amber among them. I'd caught amber fever on my first trip to Tallinn in 1988. I bought my first strand of the translucent whiskey-shaded stones in irregular shapes from a street vendor for next to nothing (and then paid a king's ransom to restring it, replacing the sewing thread with jewelry wire at home).

Most of today's Baltic amber is harvested in Kaliningrad, and I treasure a necklace of what was called milk amber that my hosts at the conference there gave me as a thank-you gift. It's made of flat disks of very pale shades of yellow. I've never seen anything like it.

But my *piece de resistance* is a robin's egg-sized chunk of striated amber with a flower trapped in the fossilized resin. I bought it in St. Petersburg for considerably more than that first strand in Tallinn. It's a dazzler that opens the conversation to lots of Russian storytelling whenever I wear it.

But I never got to see the most dramatic presentation of the gemstone, the Amber Room at Catherine Palace at Tsarskoye Selo near St. Petersburg. In the early eighteenth century, German artisans worked sheets of amber set in gold leaf into wall-sized panels for a palace in Berlin. The amber-walled room was then given to Peter the Great to cement a political alliance, and it was reconstructed at

Catherine Palace. It awed visitors there until the Siege of Leningrad during World War II.

Just ahead of the Germans, desperate curators tried to separate the panels from the walls but they proved too brittle. So they plastered ordinary wallpaper over the amber in hopes of hiding it. Not so easily fooled, the Germans sent in a team of art restorers who removed the amber panels to a vault near Konigsberg where, irony of ironies, the advancing Red Army is said to have destroyed them in an artillery onslaught in 1945.

Much like the sightings of the Swedish diplomat Raoul Wallenberg, treasure hunters have followed leads all across Europe on the trail of those amber panels—without success. Russia launched an effort to replicate the Amber Room at Catherine Palace in 1979, and I saw it in mid-progress in 1990. The finished chamber was dedicated in 2003 as part of the three-hundredth anniversary celebration of the city of St. Petersburg.

I loved the hotel in Riga, but I got a kick out of the little drama that greeted me when I arrived. A Russian couple ahead of me was trying to check in, but the receptionist kept protesting that she didn't understand them, that people in Riga spoke Latvian, not Russian. But when I stepped to the counter, presented my American passport and said, "*Po-angliyski ili po-russki?* (In English or in Russian?)"

In Russian, she replied. It's better than my English.

Just four years after their independence, Latvians were no more ready to forgive and forget their forced Russification than the Estonians had been. Like it or not, this young woman had been compelled to study Russian in school, but now she was in a position to demand that Russians speak Latvian to her.

Not sure how her employer felt about it, but she was pretty smug.

I'D BEEN AWAY from e-mail the whole time I was in Riga so I was particularly happy to hear the chirpy "You've got mail!" when I flipped open my laptop back in my flat. My flash session to download my inbox took several minutes so I made myself comfortable on my bed with the laptop while I waited. I wanted to hear that Robyn was settled in New York. Every passing thought of her still raised goose bumps on my arms and called up that gut punch of worry that had nearly scuttled me when she'd gone missing in Germany.

But the big news came from church friend Mike Venturino, the United captain. I'd e-mailed him my arrival information as soon as I made my airline reservations to see if he could pick up Laurie's Voyager van from the house in San Mateo and meet my plane at SFO to haul all my bags and boxes home. No problem, but he added that he had almost a week between trips about the time I would be traveling. If I'd like, he could jump-seat on Lufthansa to Moscow, help me pack up those ten boxes and bags and then fly back with me. He would get someone else to meet us with the van.

Yes, yes, yes! I slid back into the big square European pillows and closed my eyes in relief. I wouldn't have to do this all alone after all.

ON MY LAST day at the Press Center, I carried a cardboard box upstairs to my tiny office with the same tattered once-white curtains (I'd meant to replace them but never quite got around to it) and flaking urine-yellow paint. The wall-sized map of the former Soviet Union was already gone. I'd removed the pins marking more than twenty Russian cities I'd visited in the past year, rolled it up and carried it home on the Metro days before.

I tucked my "office" pumps for my Mr. Rogers routine into the box with all the Russian newspapers I'd used as fodder for the design manual. The Society of News Design yearbooks that Valerie had shipped over would remain in the Press Center library, and my desktop computer, scanner, printer, and modem would all go to Nick Pilugin, another USIA operative with an office (often shared with short-term PIRs) down the hall.

Nick had been a great resource. He and his wife had lived in Moscow for years with Nick shifting from one NGO grant to another. Theirs was a true ex-pat existence. Moscow was their home, and trips to the States were just visits. He looked like an American with his long ponytail and John Wayne stride, but he navigated Moscow like a native. He grew up in a Russian-speaking home in the Midwest, and he was the go-to guy for help in finding anything in Moscow.

Last winter, Nick had an interview with a newspaper editor in Obninsk, Russia's Science City, and he asked if I'd like to come along. It's about seventy miles southeast of Moscow, and we made it a day trip. I was game to explore this forty-year-old planned metropolis, which, I'd been told, was dying young.

In a country of thousand-year-old cities with stone *kremli* (fortresses) and onion-domed cathedrals, Obninsk has no *kremlya,* and the closest thing to a cathedral is the meteorological tower ("the highest in the world!"), which can forecast weather across the entire Volga-to-Danube plain (could it be cold, damp, and gray?).

This city was home to the world's first nuclear power station at Beloyarsk in 1956. Obninsk was to be clean and safe, built around this revolutionary graphite-moderated nuclear reactor that would become the model for scores of others around the Soviet Union and its puppet states—including Chernobyl in Ukraine. You can date the beginning of the end of Obninsk to April 26, 1986, the day reactor No. 4 at Chernobyl melted down in the world's worst technological accident.

Science, any citizen on any Russian street would tell you, now was the most underfunded facet of Russian society. University professors went unpaid for months at a time. Government grants for research had dried up, and private western foundations were the primary sources for scientific funding.

The resulting brain drain was nowhere more evident than in Obninsk. Perhaps most degrading of all, many of these boarded-up institutes, once dedicated to the pursuit of pure science, now served as conference sites for *biznesmen* who came to Obninsk to see what technology they could cart away.

The Sister City of Oak Ridge, Tennessee, Obninsk had no illusions about its future, and residents were bitter. The editor we visited promised to take me to the "ruins" of the nuclear reactor.

"From reading the papers in Moscow, you'd think it's a radioactive hulk and everyone in Obninsk is glowing, but it's still providing energy for this entire region. We keep looking to Moscow to recognize what they are wasting here, but there's never an answer.

"We've lost our voices, and they've lost their hearing."

A week later, the editor wrote a column about our visit, and he detailed much of what Nick had to say—between snarky comments about his ponytail and his less-than-perfect Russian grammar. He had not one word to say about my presentation, but he did note that I reminded him of an aging Claudia Schiffer. Ouch!

I stacked up all my computer user manuals and desk paraphernalia and carried them down to Nick's office. Feet propped on his desk, he was chatting away in Russian on the phone (he was always on the phone) but he nodded his thanks.

PLEASE JOIN US in the library for a hundred grams of tea, Svet said, as he swept his arm toward the door of my office to usher me out. I could count on one hand the number of times he had come up the stairs to talk to me and, as always, he was very formal and perhaps a bit edgy. If he just needed me for something, he would have sent the *dezhurnaya* with the message, so this was no casual invitation.

The library was packed with twenty-something interns, Press Center staff, newspaper editors, and friends, all standing and clapping when I walked in. The tears that always welled near the surface these days spilled over as Alan Dodge put his arm around me and led me to a chair by the window. Platters of sweet and savory treats covered every flat surface, and tea was hardly the beverage of choice.

This RAPIC family of mine was sending me off in style—part tribute (the first copies of the design manual were on display) and part roast (Nick couldn't resist sharing the Claudia Schiffer zinger!). Then Svet put a small but very heavy package in my hand.

"We have a small piece of Russia for you to take home to hold your Russian soul."

I peeled away the wrapping to reveal a spectacular stone vase, perhaps three inches tall, made of charoite, a rare purple mineral swirled with veins of black and flecks of white that can be found in just one place in the world, not far from the Chara River near Lake Baikal in Siberia. I had seen gorgeous charoite bead necklaces but such a large piece, so perfect and dense, took my breath away.

"They say it will all be gone in a few years," someone chimed in, retelling the (possibly true) story that a truckload of it went to tile the bathroom of Gorbachev's highly unpopular wife Raisa.

A tangible piece of Russia for me to take home: I had stored up a year's worth of intangibles, but this was stunning testimony to my most difficult year.

The RAPIC going-away party with Alan Dodge.

I WAS WORRIED about the rugs I was bringing home. Although taking carpets from Azerbaijan and Turkmenistan (bargains from the outdoor market at Izmailovo) out of Russia was perfectly legal, Customs officials could be quirky. Lots of Western friends told horror stories about having rugs or paintings or jewelry snatched away at the last minute and getting caught in enough bureaucratic snafus to make them miss their flights.

Just to make sure, I'd hired Gennady to drive me and the five rugs (two room-sized wool ones and three smaller silk ones) to the ministry office where I could obtain an *expertiza*—a document to prove that the items in question could legally be exported from Russia, that the rugs were not valuable antiquities that I'd bought (probably in good faith) from thieves.

Getting an *expertiza* involved wading into serious Russian red tape (think Dickens' Circumlocution Office in *Little Dorrit*) but I was feeling a bit guilty, not for these rugs, but for an icon I'd bought from a street vendor on Stariy Arbat on my first trip in 1988. It never occurred to me when I paid a few thousand rubles for it that it might be authentic, but after I got home, I heard about the wholesale raping of village churches when valuable icons were lost forever. No Stateside appraiser could give me a definitive answer, but they all agreed that mine was very old and might well have been chiseled off an Orthodox *iconostasis*.

So into the bureaucratic maw with barrel-chested Gennady as my bearer! After two false starts (which, miraculously did *not* involve car trips across the city), we found the right office. I endured the usual queue, shoving the bundle of rugs along the splintering parquet floor with my foot.

These are rubbish, the clerk hissed at me. You are wasting my time!

She had a lot more to say, enough to make Gennady blush, but I still wanted my *expertiza*. I wanted to be properly armed in case I caught a Customs inspector in the mood for games. When it was clear I wasn't going to carry my throwaway rugs off without a piece of paper, the clerk harrumphed, recorded her opinion ("worthless") and affixed the ministry's official stamp.

Now I was happy. Russians love official stamps, and I was thrilled to have one handy just in case. I know I embarrassed Gennady (I caught him rolling his eyes). The afternoon in search of the *expertiza* will no doubt get proper attention when he writes his memoir, *Driving the Amerikanka!*

MIKE WAS AS good as his word. Two days before my flight home, he arrived to help pack my rugs and empty my flat of all those things I'd brought to create a home here on the *naberezhnaya* of the

Moscow River—the photos from the top of the piano, the pressed roses from Laurie's anniversary bouquet, the red lacquer box with the Firebird on the lid, Bette's scarf, and the big square European pillows and comforter.

I'd already taken down the screening I'd tacked to my windows to keep the mosquitoes out and unwittingly opened a bidding war for it at the Press Center. (One of the interns won.) The toaster and coffee grinder I'd bought in Moscow went to Tanya, and I was pleased to make a gift of the vacuum cleaner to my neighbor who had clucked over me non-stop for the past two months.

As I emptied the bottom drawer of my *shkaf*, I pulled out the thick manila envelope with information about Raoul Wallenberg that my Congressman, Tom Lantos, had entrusted to me almost exactly a year before. Only then did I remember the appointment I'd made with the official records administrator at the Russian State History Museum on Red Square. My Cox News colleague, whom I'd met in the hallway at Spaso House months ago, had suggested that this man might have something new to add to the Wallenberg mystery. On the phone, he'd assured me he did not, but he would be happy to show me the data supporting the opinion that Wallenberg died in prison in 1957. We'd made the appointment for Monday, July 31, but I was standing on the banks of the Clark Fork of the Tuolumne River in California that day.

I knew that Lantos would understand, but it was a mission left undone, all the same. I sat back on the floor, leaning against the bed and absorbing a wave of regret.

MY LAST NIGHT in the flat, Alan Dodge, Renny Hart, and a couple other interns brought *shampanskoye* to celebrate the rehanging of the ugly orange sateen drapes. But it would have to be a short night since Gennady in his Lada and Svet in his Moskvitch would be coming at 4 a.m. to get Mike and me to the airport in time for the seven o'clock Lufthansa flight to Frankfurt.

Everyone left early with many tears and hugs and promises to stay in touch. I walked them down to the *naberezhnaya*, hidden by a blanket of new snow, for a last goodbye. Then I stood alone in the courtyard, with my head tilted up and eyes closed, to catch some snowflakes on my cheeks and eyelashes for some time before I went in. The last day of my Great Adventure was done.

In the pitch dark of the early morning, Mike and I helped load the bags and boxes into and on top of the two cars parked in the darkness behind my building. Then I went back upstairs alone and sat quietly on that rock-hard velveteen couch in the living room for a few minutes, in the Russian tradition before a journey, to collect my thoughts and make sure I had everything I needed. For Russians, it's stupendously bad luck to run back in to pick up something forgotten after you're on your way. Most will go without it before they'll run the risk of going back in again.

At Sheremetyevo, the Customs inspector proved to be much more interested in a cheap acrylic landscape of a wispy pink winter sky than my rugs, but he agreed that this painting was not great art. As for the carpets, he didn't even open the boxes! I was crushed. That hard-won *expertiza* with embossed ministry stamps had all gone for naught.

Getting Lufthansa to accept those ten boxes and bags had kept me awake nights as well. I had done all the paperwork in alerting the airline to the overage and had even spent an afternoon going to the Lufthansa office—two buses, the Metro, and a hike across that muddy construction site next to Olimpiyskiy Stadion—to show them the GEBATS (government excess baggage coupons) USIA had issued to me. I'd called five days before, to tell them the size and weight (in centimeters and kilograms), and then again the day before I was to leave to make sure it was confirmed. But this was all old hat to the airlines. They'd been schlepping diplomats and NGO workers and their households in and out of the country for years, and my ten bags barely made a dent in the hold of a 747. For Lufthansa, not even a hiccup!

I had reason to be smug now since I knew my visa and passports were in order. I had just used them both the week before on the train trip to Riga when I had spent my next-to-last exit and my last entry. Mike and I were already tasting the good German coffee on the plane when he passed through the Passport Control gate and I stepped up to the window. I remember remarking to myself that the smart-looking young woman who took my *dokumentii* was smiling, a dramatic change from my first trip to the Soviet Union in 1988.

She was still smiling when she handed them back, saying, "This is not a visa any more, only a record of your visa. Please step aside."

I was no longer smug, in fact, I was trying desperately not to cry as my Russian deserted me in my panic. Mike watched wide-eyed from the other side of the gate, from "outside" Russia, but I was still inside—and they really weren't going to let me leave. After nearly a year of what everyone considered "good works," they weren't going to let me go home. After I had willingly returned to finish my project two months earlier, even after the trauma of my husband's death, they weren't going to let me go.

I pleaded, explaining that the number of exits and entries were correct—three of each—and I even counted the stamps for them to show I was right. When I pointed to a hotel stamp precariously close to the space for one exit, everyone agreed that the immigration officer on the train from Riga, in the pre-dawn darkness, had mistaken that for an exit and considered the visa expired. She had torn off the main portion of the visa and, along with it, my opportunity to leave Russia with Mike and my ten pieces of baggage.

Yes, a mistake, but that didn't alter the fact that I no longer had a valid visa.

The Lufthansa agent was sympathetic but her concern was for the excess baggage, which was already in the hold of Lufthansa Flight 3132. Would the gentleman take it? We shouted across the gate back and forth. Yes, of course, he would take it and see me in San Francisco. Miserably, we waved goodbye.

Now my only hope rested with the Russian consul who had an office at the airport. The agent explained that he had the authority to issue me a new exit visa, but there was no guarantee. He might, and he might not. If not, I'd have to return to Moscow and slog through the bureaucracy to get one. Ah, Russia! I had managed to suspend my passion for logic for nearly a year, but I was having a rough time now.

So I sat in no-man's land between Customs and Passport Control on a metal baggage conveyor at an unused check-in counter in tears. I would wait for two hours until the consul would get in and try to imagine what tack I would take. Would I plead? Beg? Cry? Demand? Ask to call my contacts at the U.S. Embassy (what contacts?)

Turned out, it didn't matter. The Lufthansa agent returned to tell me she had spoken to the consul, and he was willing to issue me a one-day visa—for one hundred and fifty U.S. dollars, twice the going rate! Hey, it was only money! I fumbled under my sweater to pull off my money belt.

Nine long hours later I boarded the next flight to Frankfurt and was booked on the next day's non-stop to San Francisco. I would have to spend an expensive three-hundred-dollar night at the Frankfurt airport hotel, but I was finally going home.

I was traveling light with my computer bag and one overnight bag. Mike now had the baggage tags for the ten bags and boxes (covered by my GEBATS) attached in a long ribbon to his ticket envelope. And he had to change planes in Frankfurt. There would have been no issue if he'd been traveling on a regular ticket, but he was using an interline pass as a United employee. The Lufthansa people in Frankfurt accused him of abusing his privilege with all the luggage. Even though the agent in Moscow had wired Frankfurt about the last-minute baggage shift, Frankfurt agents weren't buying it. Mike, who doesn't suffer fools gladly, was treacherously close to jeopardizing his job when they finally waved him through.

In San Francisco, another crisis over those bags awaited him— and he knew it. All those bags had my identification details plastered all over them. Explaining how he happened to have them and why he should be allowed to bring them through U.S. Customs wasn't going to be simple—even though he had the appropriate baggage stubs.

He retrieved all the bags and boxes and loaded them onto three carts. (It'd taken me four carts when I arrived at Sheremetyevo a year ago, but the SFO carts must have been sturdier.) He shuttled them along, one after another, until he was facing one very skeptical Customs agent who listened to his tale. The agent called over to a co-worker.

This guy says all these bags belong to Michelle Carter, a journalist who's been living in Moscow for a year. Do you know anything about that?

Michelle Carter, he said. Oh, yeah, she's the one who's been writing the *Letters From Russia* in the *San Mateo Times*. Guess she's coming home.

AND SO I was.

Laurie's Voyager van carried the bags and boxes back to the house where they waited in the living room until I showed up with my two little carry-on bags from the flight from Frankfurt the next day. My cats, who'd been cared for by a house sitter for most of the last two months, wanted to be aloof to punish me for my absence, but those cartons got the best of them. They both scrambled up on them and sniffed around until I got a kitchen knife and sliced the boxes open.

I pulled out one of my "worthless" rugs and spread it out on the hardwood floor. The cats were on it in an instant, rolling around and rubbing their jaws on the pile, moaning and grunting. Surely they smelled the camels that carried them from Turkmenistan (at least in my imagination)! My return was no big deal for the cats but, oh, those rugs . . .

I left the cats to their carpet ecstasy and walked through the empty house, finding my grief neatly folded and stacked, like laundry, waiting patiently for me to come back to it. Those two months in Moscow had been an interlude, an interruption, but now it was time to get down to the serious work of going on alone—without my children, without a job, without health insurance, without Laurie.

Still in my navy blue coat with the brass buttons, much too warm for California, I stood in front of the sink in the tiny bathroom off our bedroom. With my finger on the mirror, I traced my sunken cheekbones, the dark circles under my eyes and blotches on my skin. I'd put on an unfamiliar costume, and I didn't know the role I was supposed to play.

No script. No plot. No plan.

Now what?

Epilogue

TWENTY YEARS HAVE passed since I stood in that empty house. It's taken twenty years for me to put that year of my Great Adventure in focus.

Robyn and David lowered a ladder into the pit where I was wallowing just a few weeks later. They both decided life on the other coast wasn't for them and launched a cross-continental road trip in David's well-worn Honda that brought them home before Christmas. As long as they were close by, I could keep on keeping on.

That Christmas, I chose one of Laurie's ties as a gift for each of his close friends, remembering the comfort that Bette's scarf had given me in my Moscow flat. Two of his long-sleeved Oxford-cloth shirts still hang in my closet. His scent is long gone, but a glimpse of them is a daily reminder.

On January 2, one year after I first arrived in Moscow, my USIA handler Valerie e-mailed me with news of a U.S. Agency for International Development grant to bring newspaper professionals in advertising, circulation, design, and management to Russia to spend two or three weeks with a single newspaper—under my direction. I could design the program with the help of RAPIC in Moscow to fit the agenda I'd found effective in the past year. Best of all, the grant was open-ended and renewable on an annual basis. Now I had a job I could direct from home that would take me back to Russia three or four times a year.

As the cherry on top, AID was interested in at least one more booklet, this one on newsroom management.

Unfortunately, the grants would provide health insurance only while I was in-country so that particular gap remained firmly in place until Laurie's and my friend Mike Venturino, the United captain, became my husband a year later. Our long family friendship blossomed into love and my second successful marriage. When we told the kids, Robyn suggested that we didn't need a wedding. At our age, we should just move in together. David jumped in. "You don't get it! Travel benefits!"

And health insurance! I could add.

Just when the frequent trips to Russia were starting to wear on me, I was offered a job as adviser to the student newspaper at a small Catholic university within walking distance of our house. That launched a delightful twelve-year career teaching journalism and communication classes at Notre Dame de Namur University of Belmont that allowed me to stretch myself again.

In 2001, Robyn gave birth to our grandson Ezra, and Mike and I were thrilled to bring him home from the birthing center (above a bail bond store in San Francisco!) in Laurie's Voyager van. He's been raised on Grandpa Laurie stories so he could know the grandfather he would never meet. Mike skipped children and went directly to a grandson he adores.

Robyn, now a published fiction writer with a masters in fine arts in writing, teaches those skills to third-through-fifth graders at Reading School in San Francisco's Tenderloin. Each student produces a book during the class, and those books (which fill the classroom library) are the ones the kids most often want to read.

David, with a master's degree in urban education, is a gifted middle and high school administrator, curriculum designer, and mentor to teachers in Oakland's charter schools.

Tanya Patina emigrated to Toronto, Ontario, with her husband and son, and now holds dual Canadian and Russian citizenship. She took her bundle of PhDs and got a job at the University of Toronto as a "risk management" specialist, a most un-Russian profession. One of those incredibly strong Russian women, Tanya is a survivor who shape-shifts to fit into the world she finds—with wit and grit.

Oleg and Elena and their children enjoy a comfortable professional life in Moscow with an apartment on the Garden Ring, and Anna Sharogradskaya continues to run her press institute in St. Petersburg, where she takes pride in spitting in the eye of authorities who challenge her right to encourage the few remaining threads of a free press in Russia.

Looking back now, Anna and I agree that the time we spent together was magical—and unspeakably fragile. Russia's flowering of *perestroika* and *glasnost* in the mid-nineties launched a bold corps of journalists who were unflinching in rooting out corruption and championing honest governance—despite the absence of a professional framework to support them.

In 1995, we believed we were helping to build a free and independent press that would speak truth to the most awful power. It was a heady dream in a china teacup that shattered under Putin's hobnailed boot.

A few brave hearts soldier on. A plucky newspaper in Siberia's Yakutia region, the *Yakutsky Vecherny* (Evening Yakutsk) prints this warning at the bottom of its television listings: "Beware. TV news programs often contain distorted or false information. The state TV channels NTV and Rossia are guilty of this more than the others." But fighting the good fight is becoming increasingly futile in this new era of smothering, state-controlled media.

But it really was all over by 2006. The end is marked by the obituary of Anna Politkovskaya, a New York-born journalist for *Novaya Gazeta* who was murdered in the lift of her Moscow flat that year, not far from mine on the Rostovskaya Embankment. Five men went to prison for her murder, but the Russian journalism fraternity knows she died because she poked her finger in Putin's eye one too many times.

In 2004, she wrote in an article, published in Britain's *Guardian*, "We are hurtling back into a Soviet abyss, into an information vacuum that spells death from our own ignorance . . . If you want to go on working as a journalist, it's total servility to Putin. Otherwise, it can be death, the bullet, poison, or trial—whatever our special services, Putin's guard dogs, see fit."

And then she was dead—along with the profession she served.

The Russian American Press and Information Center in the yellow building on Khlebny pereulok disappeared within a year after I came home. Russia's crackdown on non-governmental organizations and the requirement to register and open its books was more than it and its American support teams cared to bear.

It's easy now to think that the wonder of this place and time was produced by smoke and mirrors, but I know better. For one year, it was my stage and my touchstone, the eastern anchor for my Great Adventure—Laurie's great gift to me.

Michelle Carter is a professional journalist with a thirty-year career in daily newspapering (*The Kansas City Star* and *The San Mateo Times*) and a twelve-year stint as a journalism instructor at Notre Dame de Namur University in Belmont, California. A graduate of the University of Missouri School of Journalism, she has been writing professionally for most of her adult life. *From Under the Russian Snow* is the second book to grow out of her experiences in the former Soviet Union. The first, *Children of Chernobyl: Raising Hope From the Ashes*, was co-written with Michael J. Christensen and published by Augsburg Publishing of Minneapolis. Carter has two children, a daughter (a published short story writer), a son (a teacher and school administrator), and a grandson (an avid blogger). A magazine editor, she lives in the San Francisco Bay Area with her husband, a retired airline captain and flying instructor, and their cat. Life is good.

Book club discussion guide

Author Michelle Carter promises to be present at book club discussions of From Under the Russian Snow, either in person or by telephone, Skype or Facetime. Contact her through the website, FromUndertheRussianSnow.org.

Discussion topics
- How is a memoir different from journalism in which the author made her career? Both genres are true, but a memoir falls into a category called literary non-fiction. Can you recall some examples where the narrative transcends journalism?
- The author writes in great detail about events that happened more than twenty years ago. Does that add depth and detail or does it cause you to suspend belief?
- The author was a fifty-year-old American woman living and traveling alone in Moscow. What kind of issues does that raise in you as a reader? Was she brave, foolhardy or perhaps just lucky?
- The author writes that the Russian press was flowering in that post-Soviet, pre-Putin bubble of freedom. How does that contrast with your understanding of the current situation in Russia?
- The author shares her indecision about going back to Russia after her husband died. Can you understand why she did?
- At one point, the author characterizes her decision to accept the position in Russia as greedy and self-centered. Could you have made a similar choice? If not, why not?
- The author draws her title from the *podsnezhnik,* the first flower to poke through the snow in the early Russian spring. Is it an apt metaphor for this memoir?
- The author is fairly critical of the treatment of women in Russia. How does this differ from the way women are treated in the rest of the world?
- A number of different themes are woven through this memoir. How did they speak to you? Were they effective in advancing the narrative? How have your perceptions about Russia changed after reading the book?